As the Child of an Alcoholic

What Hope Is There for Us Damaged Folks?

Wayne and Tamara Mitchell

Contents

Acknowledgements   V

Epigraph   VII

1. Introduction   1

2. Three Children   3

3. An Outdated Book   7
   The Story Behind The Book
   Enabling Defined
   Generalizations About Children of Alcoholics

4. Two Underlying Ideas   11
   Self-regulation
   Executive Functioning
   The Dysfunctional Home

5. That-Which-Must-Not-Be-Named   19
   Child Maltreatment
   Developmental Risks
   The Building Block Period
   Adverse Childhood Experiences
   What Must Be Named

6. Trauma   27

7. Complex Trauma   29

    Complex PTSD
    When Complex PTSD Is Most Severe
    Implications for Children of Alcoholics

8. What Needs Healing   33
    Compensatory Mechanisms of Children of Alcoholics
    Common Mental Issues in Children of Alcoholics
    Trauma
    Depression
    Borderline Personality Disorder
    Dissociation
    Downside of 'Positive' Fantasies

9. 'Great Parents'   39
    Effects of Prolonged Exposure to Trauma

10. Facing Facts   43
    Grieving Losses
    Losses of Maltreated Children
    Overcoming Unresolved Grief

11. The Nervous System, Part 1   47
    Bruce Perry's Model of the Nervous System

12. The Nervous System, Part 2   51
    Three Pathways of Response

13. Shame   55
    Understanding Shame
    Flipping the Shame Script

14. Recalibration, An Overview   59
    Phases of Recovery
    Professional Help

       The Therapy Experience
       Focusing on Gains

15. Asking For Help   65
       Wayne's Experience
       What to Expect

16. Boundaries   71
       Boundaries Defined
       Guidelines for Setting Boundaries

17. Understanding Yourself   79
       Suggestion One: Put Order In Your Day
       Suggestion Two: Persist, Even When Progress Seems Slow
       Spend Your Energy on Healing

18. Alcoholics Anonymous   83
       The Nature of AA
       The Disease Concept of Alcoholism
       Addiction Defined
       How To View Alcoholics

19. Enablers And Bonding   89
       Animal Research
       Human Research and Styles of Attachment
       Secure Attachment
       Types of Insecure Attachment
       What Children of Alcoholics Need

20. A Deeper Look At Enabling   95
       Enabling and Children
       Risk and Enabling
       Enablers Fail to Protect Children

      Codependency

21. Adult Children of Alcoholics®   105
      The Problem With Adult Children of Alcoholics
      Failures of Adult Children of Alcoholics
      The Illusory Truth Effect
      The Motives of Toxic Parents

22. Helpful Apps   111
      Untold
      How We Feel
      InnerWorld

23. Conclusion   115

A Brief Note   117

About the authors   118

Resources   119

Chapter Notes   121

References   128

Acknowledgements

Special thanks to Susan Voskuil and Nadya Yayla for their thoughtful suggestions on an earlier version of this manuscript. We are indebted to them for their assistance.

"Men's courses will foreshadow certain ends, to which, if persevered in, they must end. But if the courses be departed from, the ends will change."
—Charles Dickens, A Christmas Carol

Chapter 1

Introduction

This book is about the damage done to children by alcoholics. If you are the child of an alcoholic, we wrote this book specifically for you.

It doesn't matter if you are young person still at home, or if you are 20, 40, or 60 years past living with an alcoholic adult. What happened to you must still be an issue or you wouldn't be here.

In *As the Child of an Alcoholic*, we offer a framework for understanding what happened to you, and we offer a way out.

Along the way, we will not advance the cause of any organization that deals with alcoholics. Our only concern is you as the child of an alcoholic. Our only desire is to help you get past the bad things that happened to you as a child.

You may have grown up with one alcoholic, multiple alcoholics, one enabler, or a succession of enablers. But when we talk about the alcoholic family, we know you can read between the lines and see how what we say applies to your own situation.

In the book, we sometimes use the word 'drunk' in place of 'alcoholic.' We do this for a reason. The word 'alcoholic' is a euphemism, and euphemisms sanitize problems. Sanitizing a problem masks it and masks the severity of it. The word 'drunk' expresses the unvarnished truth as lived by children of alcoholics.

Courts and the law understand this unvarnished truth. They don't knowingly allow a child to be adopted in a family where one or both parents are alcoholics. They understand that an alcoholic and an enabler in a child's life are a blight.

A blight doesn't kill, it impairs.

Finally, let us make a note about terms. Today there is no diagnosable condition called alcoholism. The U.S. National Institute on Alcohol Abuse and Alcoholism calls the word 'colloquial.' The current medical term is Alcohol Use Disorder, or AUD.[1]

The word 'alcoholism,' however, survives in popular usage and in the language of some groups, like Alcoholics Anonymous. Out of necessity, we use the term, but it is out of date.

For 22 years, we wrote an advice column. During that time, we answered hundreds of letters from children of alcoholics. In this book, we share some of those personal stories, as well as findings from scientific research.

Wayne is the child of an alcoholic; Tamara is not. But this book is from both of us, in equal measure.

Chapter 2

Three Children

> If you can look into the seeds of time,
> And say which grain will grow and which will not...
> —Shakespeare, *Macbeth*

Let us introduce three people, each the child of an alcoholic. The first person, a man, wrote us after seeing one of our newspaper columns. The subject line of his email was 'Constant Feeling of Dread.'

I just read your response to a woman married to an alcoholic and was wondering if you could help me.

Your answer stated in part that "children raised in this environment often become people pleasers who judge themselves harshly and have a hard time following through on projects. They likely will have difficulty disclosing their feelings to others, and they likely will live with a constant feeling of dread."

I am now 34, live alone, and have never been married. I grew up in a household where my father worked unbelievable hours and my mother drank every night. She was fine during the day, but her mood would change every night after drinking several glasses of wine.

She would lash out at me and my other siblings, a.k.a. 'the rotten kids', for just about any reason and would often start crying for no apparent reason. When I was younger, I would ask her what was wrong and try to cheer her up. As I got older, I avoided talking to her after dinner for fear of upsetting her and getting into an argument.

Until my teens, I never understood why she acted that way and sincerely believed she didn't love me. Over the years, my siblings and I tried to talk to her, but neither she, nor my father, will admit there is a problem. Each night she and my father (who is now retired) eat dinner, watch TV, and drink.

I would love to see her stop drinking, but without my father's support, I don't believe it will be possible.

My question for you is this. I lost my job as a corporate attorney at a large law firm, and despite a concerted effort to find another job in the legal field, I am still unemployed. I feel I have become the person you described, i.e., a people pleaser who judges himself harshly and lives with a constant feeling of dread.

Despite having graduated at the top of my class from an elite university and law school, I don't feel worthy of being hired.

That may sound strange, but I don't feel I have anything to offer. In general, I am so worried about doing the wrong thing I end up doing nothing. The parttime work I've been doing isn't paying the bills, and I'm running out of savings. I want to get my career back on track, if not in the legal profession, then somewhere else.

Do you think my childhood experience with my mother could be related to my current feelings and employment situation? If so, are there any books that you could recommend? Thank you.

Frank

A friend of ours told us about one of her friends:

My friend Leah grew up with a drop-to-the-floor-drunk alcoholic mother, who finally was hospitalized and eventually got sober. One day, Leah commented to our mutual friend Alice and me, that she loved having a glass of wine after work each day. But every time she thought of it, she was thrown into guilt and anxiety.

Leah asked if we thought it could possibly be okay to have a glass of wine each day. When I commented her extreme anxiety might be from having had an alcoholic parent, Leah was dumbstruck. "REALLY? You REALLY think that could have something to do with it?"

One might think she was being sarcastic, as in, "DUH, like, tell me something else I don't know." But she wasn't, not at all. She went on, expressing

doubt and amazement that something that happened so long ago (in childhood) could possibly affect her in any way in late middle age.
I was equally amazed she would think for one minute that it wouldn't.

The final child of an alcoholic is Tara, a young woman studying at a British university. Tara is 25.

She says, "People who know me say I look attractive, but I feel numb and insecure." About her childhood she recalls, "There were always arguments, rage, and alcohol in my family."

Tara has been in multiple relationships, mostly with older, married men. As she explains, "I think this is because of my black childhood, the lack of love, and the lack of a nice family atmosphere."

Tara says she is from "somewhere in Asia." Her father was an alcoholic and her parents divorced when she was 15. Her older brother, an alcoholic, was married with one child. Over the course of several days, he binged on cheap vodka and drank himself to death.

"I don't understand what's going on with me," Tara says. "In general, I guess, I have lost my personality because I cannot feel who am I, what I like, what am I going to do, what I want, who I want to be, and what is my point of life? Sometimes I think it would be better to die and be out of this dirty world."

If you are the child of an alcoholic, you may be like Frank, Leah, or Tara. Or your story may be a little different. But as the child of an alcoholic, your problems stem from two basic facts.

1. The child's goal is to master reality.
2. The alcoholic's goal is to flee from reality.

This leads to an obvious conclusion. If Frank, Leah, and Tara grew up in a different home, with parents who were emotionally attuned to them, they would be different people today.

If you are the child of an alcoholic, the same is true of you.

We had a friend named Glen McCray. Glen was a child psychiatrist. He was in his 90s when we knew him, and he was a perfect gentleman, known for his impeccable good manners.

When we asked Glen about his experience with the parents of troubled children, he surprised us. He said he often wanted to leap out of his chair, grab the man and woman by the neck, and throttle them both. "They were," he said, "literally killing their child."

The key to a child's well-being, Glen told us, is to find someone in the family who actually cared about the child. Just one caring person could be enough, but, he said, he often met fathers who despised their children and mothers who were in competition with them.

Glen told us about one father who finally understood what he was putting his child through, and it had nothing to do with anything Glen told him.

Instead, the man was caught in a blocks-long traffic jam caused by an accident, when he was on his way to an urgent meeting. The man said he left his car to ask the motorists in front of him to move a little left or a little right so he could get through. But the cars were so tightly packed it was impossible for him to move ahead.

It was then the man realized that was the position his child was in. Nothing the child did or could do would help him. Children have no power, no authority, and nothing that belongs to them. They are as tightly trapped in the family as that father was in the traffic jam.

Glen McCray knew each child needs at least one advocate, and research supports him.[1] But many children of alcoholics do not have a consistent, true advocate.

In the following pages, we will share the life stories of children of alcoholics and support what we say with evidence from scientific studies. But first, let's talk about the 40-year-old book that kicked off discussion about adult children of alcoholics.

Chapter 3

An Outdated Book

> We first make our habits,
> then our habits make us.
> —Anonymous

In 1983, Janet Woititz published *Adult Children of Alcoholics*. By 1987, the book had become a New York Times bestseller, and the title passed into the language as a common phrase.

But the title has a problem. It suggests, when children of alcoholics reach legal age, traits emerge which were not there beforehand. It's as if something dropped out of the sky, fell on these children, and they suddenly became 'an adult child of an alcoholic.'

What's missing in Woititz's book is the link between the child and the adult, a link which is continuous and uninterrupted. There aren't 'adult children of alcoholics.' There are only children of alcoholics.

As Wordsworth wrote, "The child is father of the man."

The Story Behind The Book

In *Adult Children of Alcoholics*, Janet Woititz described 13 traits of children raised in alcoholic households.[1] The one thing she omitted was her own backstory.

For 20 years, Janet Woititz was married to a violent alcoholic. Their home was peppered with shouting, tears, smashed glass, and police cars in the driveway. On a daily basis, Janet's husband, a journalist and network producer in New York City, staggered home.

In 2015, Woititz's daughter Lisa published a book called *Unwelcome Inheritance*. In that book Lisa described growing up in her mother's household as "a childhood from hell."[2]

At night, Lisa sat outside her bedroom door absorbing the emotional shock of the brawling. When her mother was rushed to a hospital, Lisa and her older brother were told Janet had been in a 'car accident.' When Lisa brought a friend home and her father was passed out on the floor, Janet Woititz lied for him. Her husband, she said, had a 'bad back.'

Lisa coped by repeatedly running away from home. However, since her parents never noticed, she always returned.

As a preteen, Lisa shoplifted. At 12, she smoked, drank, and listened to her mother's lies. As she recalls, "I learned that my mother's lies were typical behavior in an alcoholic home."[3]

Eventually, Janet Woititz returned to school and divorced her husband. A little later, she wrote *Adult Children of Alcoholics*, the book that made her famous. While Janet travelled giving lectures, her daughter threw after-school keggers.

Lisa struggled to hold two pictures of her mother in her mind. On the one hand, she thought of her mother as a rock star because of her fame; on the other hand, Lisa realized her mother was a master enabler.

Enabling Defined

What is enabling? The American Psychological Association defines it as "a process whereby someone (i.e., the enabler) contributes to continued maladaptive or pathological behavior (e.g., child abuse, substance abuse) in another person."[4]

Enablers often contribute to maladaptive or pathological behavior *simply by doing nothing at all*.

Children of alcoholics often hold two pictures of their parents in their mind. The first picture is an idealized one, based on the child's needs and hopes. The second picture is truer, because it is based on the reality of living with a drunk parent and an enabler.

Generalizations About Children of Alcoholics

The following is Janet Woititz's list of "generalizations that recur" in adult children of alcoholics (ACoAs).

Adult children of alcoholics:
1. Guess what normal is.
2. Can't complete projects.
3. Lie when it's easy to tell the truth.
4. Judge themselves harshly.
5. Have difficulty having fun.
6. Take themselves too seriously.
7. Struggle in intimate relationships.
8. Overreact to change.
9. Are approval-seekers.
10. Feel different from other people.
11. Are either very responsible or very irresponsible.
12. Are loyal when it's not warranted.
13. Are confused, impulsive, and self-loathing.

As you may have noticed, Woititz's list is redundant. Items 1, 7, 9, 10, 11, and the first two parts of item 13, are aspects of the same issue. Item 4 belongs with the last part of item 13. Items 2, 5, 6, and 8 belong together. Finally, items 3 and 12 refer to the martyred obligation children of alcoholics feel to present their family as normal to the outside world.

But there is a better way to look at Wotitz's list. The whole list can be reduced to two underlying psychological concepts: self-regulation and executive functioning.

Chapter 4

Two Underlying Ideas

> "If you were neglected or abused as a child,
> your primary orientation to the world is likely
> to be one of threat, fear, and survival."
> —Arielle Schwartz, psychotherapist[1]

As we mentioned in the previous chapter, Janet Woititz's generalizations about children of alcoholics are overlapping and redundant.

That's why there is a more insightful way to discuss the problems of children of alcoholics—something was missing from their development. That missing something is best explained through two psychological concepts: self-regulation and executive functioning.

Self-regulation

Self-regulation refers to our ability to manage our thoughts and emotions to achieve goals.

Self-regulation[2] allows us to:
- control our impulses and focus on a task
- regulate intense emotions, like anger and embarrassment
- calm ourselves after something exciting or upsetting happens
- refocus our attention when finishing one task and beginning another
- behave appropriately and get along with others

To develop their brain, children need to be around mature brains—brains working from reality, brains meeting challenges and facing facts. Observing those brains and patterning themselves after them gives children what they need to thrive.

If your self-regulation is good, you can:
- resist impulsive acts that make your life worse
- act in accordance with your long-term best interests
- act according to your values
- handle your emotions

But children are not born with self-regulation. They are born with the *potential* to get it from their parents or parent figures in a process called Co-regulation.

Co-regulation refers to the way the nervous system of the parent influences the nervous system of the child.[3] Just as workmen use scaffolding to build a building, a child needs their parents to provide the emotional, social, and intellectual scaffolding they need to develop in healthy ways.

That raises a dilemma. How can a child successfully pattern themselves after a person two, three, or four times past the legal limit of drunkenness?

The answer from developmental psychology is clear. They can't. The child's nervous system will become dysregulated because, as one man said about his alcoholic father, "He was always talking out of his ass."

Equally bad, when a child interacts with an enabling parent, he or she learns to accept what the enabler accepts. And, as the American Psychological Association definition suggests, enabling is not simply about aiding the substance abuser, it is also about child abuse. So the child seeks love and a sense of belonging from a second person modeling subpar behavior.

Think of it this way.

The role of parents is to teach children the story of maturity. Without learning that story, the child will struggle throughout life. But if a child learns about maturity from warm, responsive people who model it, they can draw upon that resource all their life.

Ultimately, the story of maturity resides at the deepest levels of our brain and our body. It lives in our nervous system, where it cannot be forgotten.

Executive Functioning

The second basic concept underlying Janet Woititz's list is Executive Functioning.

Executive Functioning is a set of mental skills that gives us the ability to plan, adapt, and organize our lives, and it predicts success in all areas of life.[4]

That definition almost makes it sound like self-regulation and executive functioning are identical. They aren't, but they are closely related. The distinction researchers make is this. *Executive functioning refers to the brain processes that make self-regulation possible, while self-regulation refers to the application of those processes to our lives.*

Like self-regulation, executive functioning grows on a timeline from infancy to late adolescence. But that timeline can be disrupted by the failings of the alcoholic household.

When Janet Woititz noted that children of alcoholics take themselves too seriously, she didn't say why. It's because these children are trapped in a problem they cannot solve. They need love and a sense of safety from adults who cannot give it to them. As a result, many of these children seek to win love by becoming approval seekers.

Even worse, some of them, like Tara in the first chapter, detach from their surroundings, become numb, and never develop a sense of who they are.[5]

Children of alcoholics arrive on the planet looking for love and caring. They have no outside resources, and their genetic code says, "Look to mom and dad to meet your needs."

When those needs are not met, the child's development is derailed, and they become frustrated. Since they cannot express that frustration at the adults who govern their home, they turn the anger inside and develop a fierce inner critic. That's why they judge themselves harshly and are often filled with self-loathing.

It is a small step for a child to go from "I am not loved" to "I am not loveable." The child, of course, has little or no self-awareness about this process.

The Dysfunctional Home

Within a decade after Janet Woititz published her book, research demonstrated her generalities do not specifically identify children of alcoholics. Rather, they identify children raised in virtually any dysfunctional home.

To put it another way, if you gave Woititz's list of 13 traits to a therapist, they could not tell you this person is the child of an alcoholic. But they could tell you he or she comes from a disordered, dysfunctional home.[6]

What are the characteristics of the dysfunctional home?
- the children's emotional needs are unmet and hidden from view
- there is a code of silence about what goes on within the family
- the parents don't know what is important to each child
- the parents interfere with the child's daily functioning
- the children lack the security of structures, routines, and limits
- the family accepts harmful behavior as normal in order to keep the peace
- the image of the happy family is more important than being a happy family

Some children escape the worst effects of the Alcohol Use Disordered home. It might be because they were born before Alcohol Use Disorder dominated the household, or they might have been born after an enabling parent left the alcoholic.

Or perhaps the child escaped the worst effects because they were the favored child or found another adult to champion them. But few children of alcoholics emerge unscathed.

Most are like this woman whose husband wrote us...

I am married to a woman I love very much. I really can't see my life without her; at the same time, I can't see my life with her anymore. She comes from a family where her father was an alcoholic and divorced her mom when she was nine. My wife is a social drinker; her older sister is addicted to alcohol and prescription drugs.

Here's the rub. My wife displays the classic characteristics of an adult child of an alcoholic (ACoA). We fight all the time because she won't let me into her life. She keeps me at arm's length and will not display the love, trust, affection, appreciation, and admiration that I need and deserve in this marriage. I never thought it could be tied to her being an ACoA, until just recently.

It's starting to make sense. The more I read the more I am starting to think it affects our relationship. We have gone through endless marriage counseling. In her mind I am always wrong and the complete source of problems in our marriage. Don't get me wrong, I am no angel, but it takes two to tango.

I think we have a pretty good life together because I make a very good living, am very attentive to her needs, and help out around the house all the time. Every time I think I am doing something to make her happy, and get her to the point where she will start loving me, she doesn't.

I can't find anything that will help me understand, cope, or help her break through this.

Laurence

We told Laurence,

"We want to believe if we are good, we will be rewarded. We want to believe an attentive, helpful, loving husband will receive in return the love he shows his wife. We want to believe the world is just.

"Unfortunately, all these things are only beliefs. None of them is necessarily true. If you want a visual representation of what happened to your wife, look up foot binding and view pictures of the painfully deformed feet inflicted for centuries upon millions of girls in China.

"What your wife endured is the psychological equivalent of foot binding. Often there is little physical or emotional abuse in alcoholic homes. Instead, there is complete emotional neglect.

"Researchers are finally coming to understand the effects of neglect. Kids enduring emotional neglect may simply never bounce back.

"Children of alcoholics frequently don't understand the link between their problems with a partner, and the alcoholic home they were raised in. Your wife built defenses as a way of handling life in her parents' alcoholic home. The problem is, now that those defenses are no longer needed, she cannot let them go. . ."

If we made a list of ACoA generalizations, based on the letters we receive, the first item on *our* list would be something Janet Woititz never mentioned. Depression. Children of alcoholics—whatever their age—typically suffer from depression, undiagnosed and untreated.

Often the adult child doesn't realize they are depressed, because it feels like their natural state.

We end this chapter with a letter and answer from our column. It illustrates one way children of alcoholics struggle in intimate relationships. We called the column. . .

Alcohol's Child

I am 40 and the daughter of an alcoholic. My parents have been married 43 years and have stayed together for lack of money and because of their health. They are really great people, but it is the typical story.

The short version is, when things were going fine for me, Dad would lose his temper and be drunk. Mom, my sister, and I would end up in a neighbor's apartment. When things were going horrible, Dad would be nice. Just when I was used to walking on eggshells, he would be nice.

So, while I was young I dated plenty of men, just to have company, and did not sleep with them. I got into a pattern of being alone and not letting a man close to me. At least one man from church wanted to date me, but I couldn't do it. I have trouble making time for men.

I help out my elderly parents on a regular basis in addition to working. How do I break this pattern? It seems like I am going to have to rethink this.
Edith

Edith, in his autobiography *My Life*, Bill Clinton talks about the enjoyable train trip he took with his alcoholic stepfather to see a baseball game in St. Louis. It was the only trip they took together. Clinton also mentions the only time he and his stepfather went fishing together, and the only time they went into the woods to cut down a Christmas tree.

The former president concludes, "There were so many things that meant a lot to me but were never to occur again."[7] That's what living with a drunk is like. You hold on to the few good memories to blot out the present and give yourself hope for the future. The hoped-for future never materializes, but it enables you to ignore the bad and cling to the 10 percent which is good.

It seems odd that our minds work this way, but intermittent rewards rarely given can bind us tighter than regular rewards regularly given. That's why you think your parents are "great people."

You say you need to rethink things, and that is the first idea you need to rethink. Living in a bottle was more important to your father than his living children. Unexpected niceness in the midst of terror creates the hardest pattern to break.

If you want to know what happened to your chances for a successful marriage and children, look no further than your drunken father and enabling mother. The one thing they had to do to deserve your care in their old age, they did not do. Coming to terms with that reality is the first step in understanding your pattern with men.

Wayne & Tamara

Later, we will explain why some children of alcoholics, like Edith, call their parents "really great people." But first, we need to talk about the elephant in the room. It's the elephant alcoholics and enablers are afraid to discuss.

Chapter 5

That-Which-Must-Not-Be-Named

"An alcoholic in his cups is an unlovely creature."
—Bill Wilson, founder, Alcoholics Anonymous[1]

Most of us use the term *child abuse* in a loose way, but professionals use a more precise term. Child Maltreatment.[2]

Child Maltreatment

Child Maltreatment has two categories: abuse and neglect. The distinction between them is this. Child Abuse includes explicit actions. Child Neglect involves the absence of action.

Child abuse comes in three forms:
- physical (punching, slapping, shoving)
- emotional (insults, humiliation, threats)
- sexual (unwanted or criminal sexual behavior)

Although physical and sexual abuse get the most publicity, in the United States 75% of all child maltreatment is thought to be neglect.[3] Neglect is defined as the failure to meet at least one basic need a child has for healthy development.[4]

Neglect includes things like going through the motions of being a parent, without actually parenting.

Developmental Risks

Let's begin with facts about children of alcoholics. Between a fourth and a fifth of Americans have lived with an alcoholic relative growing up.[5] These children are at a higher risk for virtually every childhood disorder.[6] They are especially at risk for disorders involving depression, anxiety, behavior, eating, substance use, and post-traumatic stress.

As professor of pediatrics Frank Putnam says, abuse and neglect harm two basic processes in children: neurodevelopment and psychosocial development.[7]

Neurodevelopment regulates growth, and it establishes networks that relay messages back and forth between the body and the brain. Psychosocial development makes it possible for us to form a personality, learn social behavior, and grow relationships.

When psychosocial and neurodevelopment are thwarted, it causes developmental arrests.

Children suffering from developmental arrests have:
1. Less ability to deal with adversity and stress
2. Less ability to bounce back from setbacks
3. Less self-assurance and composure
4. Less openness to new experiences
5. Greater impatience
6. Greater insecurity
7. A damaged self-image

The Building Block Period

Children have sensitive periods, short periods of time during which a function or capacity is easily developed.[8] Unfortunately, once the sensitive period has passed, it may be difficult or impossible for the child to acquire what they missed.

The Centers for Disease Control and Prevention (CDC) refers to the period from before birth to late adolescence as the 'building block' period.[9] Toxic stress at this time can cause impulsive behavior and poor decision-making for a lifetime.

The CDC reports that children growing up with toxic stress will have more difficulty:
- forming healthy relationships
- establishing a stable work history
- coping with finances, family, and jobs

In addition, they are more likely to fail in school, more likely to become addicts, and more prone to violence.[10]

Adverse Childhood Experiences

In the mid-1990s, a large-scale study of child abuse and neglect was begun in California. The research was called the CDC-Kaiser Permanente Adverse Childhood Experiences study.[11] It tracked the effects of Adverse Childhood Experiences (ACEs) on adults as they moved through life.

The study included a variety of childhood stressors, such as living with someone using street drugs or living with criminals.

The rarest event in the study, found in only 3% of homes, was a child seeing their mother or stepmother threatened or harmed by a knife or gun. **The most common adverse event, found in 23.5% of homes, was a child growing up with a problem drinker or alcoholic.**

The researchers found a strong link between adverse childhood experiences and the risk of developing the following ailments in adulthood: heart disease, cancer, chronic lung disease, liver disease, skeletal fractures, and general ill health.

When psychiatrist Martin Teicher and his colleagues at Harvard Medical School examined over 180 research reports, they found "an association between childhood maltreatment and alterations in brain structure, function, connectivity or network architecture."[12]

In a similar vein, Irish researchers[13] looking at child maltreatment found the effects of abuse and neglect included all the following:

- a smaller brain (e.g., in the amygdala, hippocampus, and prefrontal cortex)
- loss of neurons and neuronal connections in the brain
- shortfalls in learning, memory, and executive function
- chronic stress-related physical and mental illness
- intensified fear and anxiety
- elevated stress hormones

Finally, the National Scientific Council on the Developing Child, another group based at Harvard, concluded that, "...building more advanced cognitive, social, and emotional skills on a weak initial foundation of brain architecture is far more difficult and less effective than getting things right from the beginning."[14]

What Must Be Named

In the Harry Potter books, the wicked Lord Voldemort is seldom called by name. Instead, he is referred to as He-Who-Must-Not-Be-Named. Alcoholics and enablers have their own version of something which must not be named.

Let's name it anyway.

Its name is child maltreatment, and it has two forms, abuse and neglect. Child maltreatment goes with alcoholic homes like butter goes on bread. It affects children in wealthy homes, children in middle class homes, and children living below the poverty line.

If you grew up in an alcoholic household, you suffered a significant Adverse Childhood Experience (ACE). And in homes where one ACE is found, there are commonly other ACEs as well.

Calling you, the reader, an adult child of an alcoholic (ACoA) doesn't begin to describe what happened to you. The beginning and early years of life are the worst time to interfere with a person's development, yet that is what routinely happens in alcoholic households.

A more descriptive name for what you endured is alcoholic child maltreatment.

As we mentioned, multiple research studies have established that there are no unique features to an adult children of alcoholics syndrome.[15] If it has no unique features, there is nothing distinctive about it. It is simply abuse and neglect.

There are no unique features to an 'adult children of alcoholics syndrome.' The traits of adult children of alcoholics are simply the effects of child abuse and child neglect.

If a child lives 8 years in such an environment, that's nearly 3,000 days. That's 3,000 days the child's nervous system is assaulted, challenged, and changed.

In concrete terms, what does all this mean? Let's listen to a woman with an alcoholic mother...

I read all the sad letters and thoughtful responses on your website, and I'm still left with some hard questions. I have the same damn story. Grew up with an alcoholic mom. Still dealing with her alcoholism while trying to live my own life.

I've been living in Nepal for the past 10 years, on and off, while she lives in Louisiana. Just lost her job because of alcoholism, actually. She recently disowned me when I married my husband. "You should have married an American," she said. "I'll never give you our house now."

Basically I have a hard time, at age 28, being honest with her about my life. I'm painfully aware of the sick cycle we go through on a monthly basis, and I'm ready to start creating boundaries so I don't have to endure this again.

I actually do want to be her friend. She's incredible when sober. I actually do want to be her daughter, despite years of being the adult. But how?

When she makes awful things happen in my life, the next day they are expected to be forgotten. Most likely she doesn't remember.

What I crave more than anything is for someone to say to me, "Michelle, learn to talk to your mom like this and this, set up boundaries like this and this, don't let her do this and this."

Then I'd try it, stick with it, and hopefully have some kind of working relationship with my mom where I don't feel guilty and deal with the effects of having an alcoholic parent on my own. Hah.

Michelle

We told Michelle…

When lawyers say they have a prima facie case, they mean the merits of the case are so obvious they can be presumed true. In a similar way, people can assume a child with an alcoholic parent is the victim of child maltreatment.

A child comes into the world fully ready to bond to a parent, and in an alcoholic, they get an adult whose behavior forces them on a maladaptive path.

At the same time the child is growing a social brain, and laying down the emotional and neurological tracks which will guide them for life, they are forced to cope with an adult incapable of fulfilling the basic role of a parent.

Like every alcoholic, your mother displays alcoholic vanity, an exalted view of herself divorced from reality. Like every alcoholic, your mother reverses the roles of parent and child and forces you to be the adult in the relationship.

Like every child of an alcoholic, you cling to the few good memories of your parent as an incredible person. What you are calling "incredible" from her is ordinary behavior from a good parent on a Wednesday afternoon.

One of the most misleading terms in the field of alcoholism is 'functional alcoholic.' The term is an oxymoron. All alcoholics are dysfunctional; they differ only in the range and sphere of their dysfunction, and in the particular people they damage.

You are still in the same relationship with her you were in when you were little. You are still trying to climb a greased pole. Even in a remote country you cannot stop her abuse.

If you had been beaten, sexually assaulted as a child, or locked in a closet for a year, you might understand this better. You are missing parenting you never had, and you want it from someone who can never give it to you.

Well-intentioned but ignorant people will want you to continue placing yourself in the way of her abuse until her actual death. We don't want that for you. We want you to see yourself for what you are: the victim of child abuse.

We are sad for that. But you must move forward, fill your life with good things, and put things in place of what you never had.
Wayne & Tamara

The basic unit of the nervous system is the neuron, and the brain has 86 billion of them.[16] Between the neurons are gaps called synapses. These synapses form pathways that allow the neurons to communicate with one another. The more one pathway is used, the more it hardens into a particular pattern of behavior. The more one pathway is used, the more it hardens into a habit.

That's why it is so hard for children of alcoholics to recover or change. To overcome the effects of maltreatment, their brain and nervous system must be rewired to form new ways of response.

A woman asked an orthodontist we knew if she should curb her child's thumb sucking. She was concerned the child's teeth might become damaged. The orthodontist told her not to worry because, "It's easier to fix teeth than it is to fix heads."

Chapter 6

Trauma

> I held my tongue, and spake nothing: I kept silence,
> yea, even from good words; but it was pain and grief to me.
> —The Book of Common Prayer

The Vietnam War lasted from 1964 to 1973[1], and nearly a quarter of all American soldiers, 700,000 troops, required psychological help to cope with their experience. However, one good thing came out of that war. It kicked off the current wave of research into neurological trauma.

As the Vietnam war dragged on, veteran 'rap groups' spontaneously formed in cities across the United States. In all, there were more than 1,200 such groups. These veterans came together not just to talk about their experience, but to talk about their symptoms.

At the time, the American Psychiatric Association lacked a category to classify the symptoms of these combat veterans, and what wasn't diagnosed wasn't treated.[2] Finally, in 1980, the American Psychiatric Association recognized post-traumatic stress disorder (PTSD) as a diagnosable condition.

This matters to children of alcoholics because their problems are similar to or identical with those of combat veterans. The main difference is that children of alcoholics fought their war behind closed doors in their parents' home.

In addition, a special kind of trauma applies to you, as the child of an alcoholic.

Chapter 7

Complex Trauma

> "There are wounds that never show on the body
> that are deeper and more hurtful than anything that bleeds."
> —Laurell K. Hamilton, *Mistral's Kiss*

In 1992, Judith Herman, a psychiatrist at Harvard, wrote a short but influential article.[1] At the time, most people considered trauma a single event, or a series of events over a short period of time. That was the familiar view of post-traumatic stress disorder.

Complex PTSD

What Herman proposed was something different. She believed the description of PTSD was inadequate because it failed to capture the effects of prolonged, repeated trauma. A key feature of prolonged trauma is the victim is under the control of someone else and unable to flee.

Judith Herman gave extended trauma a new name—Complex PTSD. In her article, she highlighted three ways prolonged trauma differs from single-incident PTSD.

The first way is in the sheer number of problems. Herman specifically mentioned:
- medical symptoms with no discernable organic cause
- a change in consciousness to avoid an unbearable reality
- a feeling of being forsaken, leading to lethargy and depression

Judith Herman wrote that Complex PTSD (CPTSD) differs from single-incident PTSD in the way it changes the personality.

In CPTSD, she said, "the psychology of the victim is shaped over time by the actions and beliefs" of the person inflicting the trauma. As a result, even when the victim escapes, they are likely to recreate a similar pathological relationship with others.

Therapist Pete Walker puts it this way. Complex PTSD is caused by "prolonged verbal, spiritual, emotional and/or physical abuse and/or neglect in childhood or elsewhere. Key symptoms are emotional flashbacks, developmental arrests and a toxic, mind-dominating critic."[2]

When Complex PTSD Is Most Severe

The UK's National Health Service reports that Complex PTSD is more severe when it occurs under these conditions[3]:
- the traumatic events happened early in life
- the trauma was caused by a parent or care provider
- the person experienced the trauma for a long time
- the person was alone during the trauma
- the person is still in contact with the party responsible for the trauma

That list fits most children of alcoholics.

In healthy families, children feel emotionally secure. They live in a virtuous cycle, where one good event creates another. But children in alcoholic families live in a vicious cycle[4].

A child hears the back door open and thinks excitedly, "Dad's home, Dad's home." When he rushes to meet his father, he realizes with disappointment, "Drunk again." Or a young teen asks her mother to go to a school event with her, and is hurt when her mother grows angry at the child for interrupting her drunken reveries.

Repeat these scenes thousands of times, and each time it injures the child. The child's nascent personality will be pulled apart or never form as it should.

If you are the child of an alcoholic, you might get a sense of the damage done to you by translating the years of your childhood into days.

- 6 years, or 2,200 days

- 8 years, or 2,900 days

- 10 years, or 3,650 days

- 14 years, or 5,000 days

- 18 years, or 6,500 days

A young man writes...

I am 21 and have finally admitted to myself that my father is an alcoholic. For years I was the one defending him against my sister, and now I understand where her anger comes from.

My father is not physically abusive, but sober or drunk, he always picks on us. Nothing is ever good enough, and we have to walk on eggshells around him. Saying the wrong thing causes him to throw a fit.

Two years ago, I was diagnosed as being severely clinically depressed, and I completed a year and a half of therapy. Now I am free of it. I dealt with my own issues but feel utter frustration, anger, and sadness at my father.

He works the nightshift, goes to the bar all day, and comes home in time to sleep an hour or two before work. We have to wake him up, which is a terrible ordeal as he yells at whoever wakes him. Sometimes he has his drunk friends at the house while my mom is at work, and they trash the kitchen.

Recently, he took my car and got drunk, then left it in an abandoned parking lot while his friend drove him around barhopping. I tracked him down to get my keys and begged him to come home with me. He laughed in my face, like it was a joke, and went off with his friend.

I do not know how to deal with this. My sadness is turning to rage, and it seems to increase every day. I am also terrified of something triggering me back into depression, and I never want to feel that kind of pain again.

Rolf

There is a saying that depression is frozen anger, and Rolf's story illustrates this. After his depression was successfully treated, his rage at being the whipping boy of an alcoholic father surfaced.

Rolf's story illustrates another basic truth for children of alcoholics, a truth so important we put it in bold.

When you have a thorn in your paw, the only cure is to remove the thorn.

Implications for Children of Alcoholics

That has two implications for children of alcoholics:
- Each day you do not act to heal the effects of abuse or neglect, you prolong them.
- The life you were meant to live is waiting for you on the other side.

When the writer J. C. Squire wrote a poem about alcoholics, he ended each stanza with the same refrain, "But I'm not so think as you drunk I am." Squire's poem expertly captures the incoherence of alcoholic speech and alcoholic thinking.

He also captured another basic truth. None of us want to deal with a drunk.

But a child?

Chapter 8

What Needs Healing

> "For some reason, we seem to believe most strongly
> in the stuff that gets into our heads without
> our knowing or remembering how it got there."
> —Verlyn Klinkenborg, author

Kids pick up on things, but they lack a mature way of understanding what they see and hear.

Growing up with a parent figure who couldn't regulate their own emotions, much less support a child's emotional growth, ACoAs feel lonely and abandoned. They were likely embarrassed about the alcohol abuse at home and embarrassed or afraid to invite friends over.

As the child of an alcoholic, you may have had a constant feeling of dread, without being able to say what you dread.

Perhaps you found a few ways of coping that seemed to help. You may have turned to perfectionism, because you wanted things to be well-ordered. Or you tried to win love by becoming a high achiever. Or you became a low achiever because you felt that is all you deserved.

You probably suppressed your feelings because you knew those feelings would upset your parents. Unconsciously you thought, "The less trouble I cause, the better it will be for everyone."

Or it may have been every man for himself in your household. Lacking deep connections in your home, you did not learn how to connect deeply with others. So today your communication with other people is on a surface level.

Finally, it could even be, though the alcoholic stopped drinking, their behavior did not change. So nothing changed for you.

Compensatory Mechanisms of Children of Alcoholics

Children of alcoholics resort to many different compensatory mechanisms to survive.

As you may know, a mantra is a word or phrase repeated over and over, often silently. Many religions make use of a mantra as a way to quiet the mind, but mantras are naturally occurring phenomena.

If you had a crippling childhood, you may have had a mantra or two rattling around in your head. One man told us he had three, which appeared spontaneously when he was a child. The first was, "I hate myself, I hate myself, I hate myself."

He told us he silently repeated that to himself millions of times. Once, in his 70s, when he checked the wrong box on a form in front of a nurse, the mantra popped out. Aloud, he said, "I hate myself."

His second mantra was "I wish I was dead" and his third was "Oh, God, please help me." He repeated these phrases again and again in childhood and later when he was an adult. He never understood where the three mantras came from, but if you grew up in an Alcohol Use Disordered home, you may share his experience.

The repetition soothes, even as it damages. The self-soothing becomes self-punishment and results in self-loathing.

Repeated mantras are only one compensatory mechanism in children of alcoholics. Developmental trauma leaves many ACoAs afraid to be involved with others. They feel lonely and disconnected, even in groups. These children from Alcohol Use Disordered homes sometimes picture themselves homesteading or living alone in a cabin in the woods.

The cabin-in-the-woods fantasy has one virtue. Without realizing it, the child acknowledges to herself that the problem is not her, but in her parents or parent figures. As one child of an alcoholic told us, "I always knew in my heart, there was nothing wrong with me. It was them."

Another child of an alcoholic told us, when he unexpectedly ran into his enabling mother in a hallway, she blurted out, "I don't know what's wrong with you." The answer, he said, appeared instantly in his brain. "You." But he held his tongue.

Knowing that it's not you, it's something that happened to you, is a key to recovery.

In Chapters 3 and 4, we discussed Janet Woititz's 13 traits of adult children of alcoholics, and we found two things underlie them. Deficits in executive functioning and deficits in self-regulation.

As you may recall, executive functioning refers to brain processes that make self-regulation possible, while self-regulation is the application of those processes to our lives.

With good self-regulation, we can plan and set goals, resist impulsive acts that make our life worse, and handle our emotions.

Self-regulation correlates with a general sense of well-being. But the chaos and stress of living with an alcoholic parent make effective self-regulation hard, if not impossible, to maintain.

Common Mental Issues in Children of Alcoholics

You can see the effects of the deficits in self-regulation by considering some of the mental issues common in children of alcoholics.

The conditions overlap and form points on a scale ranging from mild to life-destroying. We will take just four for illustration: trauma, depression, borderline personality disorder, and dissociation.

But first, a caution.

This book is an overview of problems affecting children of alcoholics. It does not provide personalized mental health or medical advice, diagnosis, or treatment.

If any problems mentioned resonate with you, you should go to a mental health or medical professional for evaluation and treatment. Reading this book is not a way to diagnose or treat mental health problems.

Trauma

The world's largest brain study of childhood trauma was conducted by researchers at the University of Essex.[1] Using AI, these scientists found evidence of disruptions in the neural networks of traumatized children—networks which are vital to self-awareness and problem solving.

The brain scans revealed three things:
1. Why traumatized children have problems with decision making
2. Why they are likely to ruminate and relive bad experiences
3. Why they may find it hard to empathize and form relationships

As researcher Megan Klabunde observed, "Even when a child who has experienced trauma is not thinking about their traumatic experiences, their brains are struggling to process their sensations within their bodies."[2] Consequently, the researchers concluded, therapists need to focus on rebuilding neural centers and the sense of self in these traumatized children.

That's another reason we dislike the term 'adult children of alcoholics.' Early intervention should be mandatory, despite what the alcoholic and enabler may want. The term 'adult children of alcoholics' pussyfoots around the issue of child maltreatment, which is central in homes with Alcohol Use Disorder.

Depression

In an earlier chapter, we mentioned that depressive disorders among ACoAs are common. As one influential study put it, "Depression among adult children of alcoholics appears to be largely, if not solely, due to the greater likelihood of having had adverse childhood experiences in a home with alcohol-abusing parents."[3]

The authors of that study noted, "Alcohol treatment programs and child protective and welfare services have tended to ignore the likelihood that they share a population of clients."

In other words, when an alcoholic enters treatment, the children typically need help for the effects of maltreatment. Research in the high income countries of Europe and North America, found that fewer than 10% of those with Alcohol Use Disorder ever get formal treatment.[4] That suggests how many children of alcoholics, trapped at home right now, need our help.

Borderline Personality Disorder

A third known problem in children of alcoholics is borderline personality disorder.

Borderline Personality Disorder (BPD) is a serious disorder involving the inability to regulate emotions.[5] Symptoms of BPD include unstable relationships and rapidly shifting moods. The symptoms may also include fears of abandonment, and a rapidly changing sense of self that causes goals, values, and behavior to waver or never become established.

When researcher Carly Porter and her colleagues in the UK analyzed 97 studies of borderline personality disorder, they found a gruesomely high connection between Borderline Personality Disorder and childhood maltreatment.[6] Neglected children are 20 times more likely to have BPD than other children, and emotionally abused children are 30 times more likely to have BPD than other children.

Dissociation

We all mildly dissociate sometimes, as when we get lost in a book or cannot remember details of our drive home from work. But for some children of alcoholics, dissociation is habitual.

Denied growth and opportunities in the real world, a child must find them somewhere, even if it is by burying their past, detaching from experience, watching themselves like an outsider, or creating multiple personalities—all of which are signs of dissociation.

Three international experts in the field—Suzette Boon, Kathy Steel, and Onno van der Hart—summarized the case simply.[7] "Dissociation generally develops when an experience is too threatening or overwhelming at the time for a person to be able to integrate it fully, especially in the absence of adequate emotional support."

Outsiders may say a dissociated child "seems to be in their own little world." For some of these children, life is like playing a role in a movie. They engage in what is called maladaptive daydreaming.

These children survive by creating a hero self in their imagination, and they create stories that are like little morality plays. In these stories the child is always smarter, braver, and wiser than anyone else.

But this alternate identity they fashion for themselves also feels like a dirty secret they can't share with others. As the behavior becomes habitual, it becomes harder and harder for them to find the present moment.

Downside of 'Positive' Fantasies

Regrettably, there is another downside to fantasy. They impair the child's (or adult's) ability to achieve goals. This is true even when the fantasies seem to be positive, like fantasizing about success.

Two researchers, one in the United States and one in Germany, conducted four experiments on the effect of positive fantasies.[8] What they found is not too surprising. Fantasies like this sap the energy needed to actually achieve goals.

As the scientists wrote, "one reason positive fantasies predict poor achievement is because they do not generate energy to pursue the desired future." They add, "Instead of promoting achievement, positive fantasies will sap job-seekers of the energy to pound the pavement, and drain the lovelorn of the energy to approach the one they like."

In short, 'positive fantasies' can have a profoundly negative effect.

All the things we mentioned in this chapter are normal compensations for the abnormality of living in an alcoholic home. In reality, children of alcoholics are normal children, bewildered, trying to weather a storm not of their own making.

Yet despite these problems, some children of alcoholics stoutly defend their inebriated parents as great parents. On the surface that's puzzling. But there is an explanation why children of alcoholics may idealize their parents. That explanation is in the next chapter.

Chapter 9

'Great Parents'

> The fiercest anger of all, the most incurable,
> is that which rages in the place of dearest love.
> —Euripides, Greek playwright

A woman began her letter this way.

I am the 49-year-old product of a violent, alcoholic home. It has taken me many, many years to let go of the shame and rage. Not to mention having to learn normal competence. At this stage, it has been my life's work...

The writer continued, asking a question about her ex-husband.

We answered her letter in our column. Near the end of our reply, we included this sentence. "You've struggled hard to find normal competence after growing up with a drunk." That was our only reference to her father's drinking, but it brought an angry reply from another reader.

She wrote:

"I am an adult child of a violent alcoholic, and I resent my father and every other alcoholic in this world being referred to as a drunk, as Wayne and Tamara did in their recent response."

She went on to admit that children of alcoholics struggle in relationships because they have "no healthy template to go by," and as a result, they may need "years and years of therapy to deal with the issues." Yet, she was offended by our use of the word *drunk*.

Her letter raises a question. Why would the daughter of a violent alcoholic defend her father so vehemently?

Perhaps this story will help explain why.[1]

In 1995, George Morgan, a convict in a Missouri prison, was doing genealogical research when he came across his little sister's death certificate. He was shocked. His sister Michelle died in 1961, and the cause of death was listed as pneumonia.

George Morgan knew that wasn't true. In 1961, he was eight and his sister four. George often saw his stepmother beat Michelle. In fact, in the last year of her life, Michelle's injuries required 24 hospital visits. Then one day George witnessed his stepmother stomp his little sister to death.

Morgan lobbied to have his sister's death reinvestigated, and ultimately, his stepmother was arrested and found liable for Michelle's death.

In the intervening years, however, the stepmother had moved to Texas and had four biological children of her own. These four children were now adults in their 30s. At their mother's sentencing for Michelle's death, they testified none of them had been mistreated. In fact, a newspaper reporter wrote that the four "seemed genuinely offended by the suggestion" their mother could hurt anyone.

Yet their medical records told a different story.

A pediatric forensic pathologist looking at the records found, as children, the four suffered "many, many, many falls" out of bunkbeds. They also suffered multiple burns and repeatedly swallowed toxic substances.

In fact, by the time they were nine, these children had 250 doctor visits, and most of the visits were before the age of four.

Effects of Prolonged Exposure to Trauma

How can we explain the testimony of the biological children? The best explanation is prolonged exposure to trauma.

In his book *Murdered Souls*, Leonard Shengold, a psychiatrist, paints a picture of children who are subjected to repeated trauma.[2] Shengold says, because the child is trapped in the family, they must register their parents "delusionally, as good."

It's as if the child unconsciously believes holding a false image of their parent is better than facing the truth.

Sometimes, also, an enabling parent is viewed as a long-suffering saint. But even then, a thorough examination of the household usually reveals their active role in child mistreatment. At times, that parent may have created more problems than the alcoholic.

Perhaps it's why Lisa Woititz said it took "lots of therapy" and deep digging for her to reach the anger she held for her mother Janet, the author of *Adult Children of Alcoholics.*

Sad to say, minimizing the injury from parents in the Alcohol Use Disordered home makes it harder to overcome the effects of being the child of an alcoholic.

Though you may want to defend your family from criticism, the reality is, as the child of an alcoholic, you suffered the most common adverse childhood experience. That's another way of saying, growing up in an AUD household was a significant piece of bad luck.

Facing facts is the best thing you can do for your recovery. That's why you need to grieve your losses. Perhaps that seems like an odd thing to say, but the explanation is in the next chapter.

Chapter 10

Facing Facts

> "Grief...is the unwelcome lodger that squats
> on the hearthstone between us and the fire
> and will not move or be dislodged."
> —Arthur Quiller Couch, writer

Because of the actions of your parents, you may have lost your chance for an education, a career, or a marriage. You might have partnered with the wrong person, stayed in the wrong job, or become the shy person who never fits into any group. Or you might be in prison.

Your unstable work history, your troubles with money, your chronic depression, your constant feeling of dread, all trace back to your caregivers. So may your awful dating history, social isolation, nervous tics, too early sex, suicidal thoughts, numbness, life on the streets, anger, aggression, and more.

These are legacies from caregivers who created deadly neural pathways in you, like the man with the mantra "I hate myself." He told us, as a child, he once asked a sibling to snap a 'gag picture' of himself. In the picture, he has a noose around his neck, with one end of the rope looped over a sturdy tree branch.

Without being able to verbalize it, he pictured what he wanted. He wanted to die.

Grieving Losses

Sadly, when abused and neglected children are told they suffer from grief, they often don't understand what that means. Another name for grief is loss. And loss, or grief, is the name for the hunger a child of an alcoholic feels for what was missing in their childhood.

Grief is a combination of sorrow, the hunger for what was missing, and anger at what should have been but wasn't.

Until you face the part of your potential that was lost to your upbringing, and mourn what cannot be recovered, you will not get over the effects of maltreatment because not facing losses is a barrier to getting better.

Until you understand the extent of your losses, and mourn them, the past will haunt you.

Therapist Pete Walker makes this suggestion.[1] Do not minimize your losses. Do not diminish or excuse what happened to you. Tally your losses and cover everything.

This is slate cleaning. Once you know what you have lost and what you can still do, you will know where you stand. When you know where you stand, you can live in reality. Living in reality will be the foundation of your new life. It will enable you to understand who you can still be.

Psychiatrist Sandra Bloom wrote, "It is exceedingly difficult to make sense of the world when you have not been cherished and protected as a child, when the very people who were supposed to love you were the people who abused, neglected, and abandoned you."[2]

Losses of Maltreated Children

In three essays Bloom wrote for *The Psychotherapy Review*, she laid out almost 20 losses maltreated children suffer from.[3]

The first thing she cited is a lack of understanding from outsiders. Outsiders don't understand how mistreated children could be mourning anything. Consequently, outsiders may think of maltreated children as 'crybabies.'

But the sense of loss in children of alcoholics is real. They often mourn a lost childhood, and possibly, the fashioning of a disastrous adulthood.

That's the first big loss. As children in an AUD home, they became hyper-aroused and dysregulated. That created an inability to manage their own emotions, which made their life much harder than the lives of other children.

Sandra Bloom also mentions these notable losses maltreated children suffer from:

- Loss of focus

- Loss of self-esteem

- Loss of a sense of safety

- Loss of suitable role models

- Loss of conflict resolution skills

- Loss of the ability to cope with overload

- Loss of the ability to stop repeating the past

- Loss of the ability to voluntarily direct attention

Not to mention the lost years of life, when the child of an alcoholic (COA) could have been someone else living a different sort of life.

Until COAs grieve their losses, they live in a counterfeit reality. They will be like Edith, who called her parents "wonderful," even though she hid from her father in a neighbor's apartment. Or they will be like Michelle, who called her drunken mother "incredible."

Children of alcoholics often face another kind of loss. They suffer from an impaired ability, or an inability, to have satisfying sexual relationships. As the wife of one COA wrote...

My wonderful, funny husband and I have been happily married for over nine years, but starting just a few months after we got married, the frequency of sex declined.

It drives me crazy, and this is our one disagreement without resolution. In desperation I cajole and use humor to try to loosen him up, with mixed results. When I try to initiate sex, he says he is tired, ticklish, not in the mood, or just wants to read or watch TV, until I forget about it.

He insists lovemaking should be spontaneous, but his spontaneity doesn't come around often enough for me!

I can't understand why he views something so pleasurable in a similar way to mowing the lawn...

Chronic, unresolved grief explains two more items on Jan Woititz's list.
Adult children of alcoholics:
- are unable to have fun and experience pleasure
- grow up feeling it is not safe to want things, so they have a hard time finishing projects

Many children of alcoholics report feeling that, though the world can be harsh, no one has ever harmed them as much as their own family.

Overcoming Unresolved Grief

We believe there are three steps to overcoming unresolved grief:
1. Acknowledging it is there
2. Understanding it is far-reaching
3. Knowing that denying your grief will only prolong it

Once you fully grieve your losses, you can cease dwelling on the past. You can focus on today and what is yet to come. When that happens, you will be free.

Unfortunately, the old ways of thinking and behaving will fight like hell not to change, because they are now wired into your nervous system as the adult child of an alcoholic.

It is important to note that part of you, as an adult child, craves the old ways. It does not want to get better. It wants to keep running down the same destructive neural pathways.

So our advice is to feel the pain, understand how the past affects every aspect of your life today, and then say goodbye to it.

But it's hard to say goodbye to the past without understanding your nervous system. Understanding the nervous system is the subject of the next two chapters.

Chapter 11

The Nervous System, Part I

> "...we literally incorporate into our bodies' cells, organs and systems the social world in which we live."[1]
> —Michelle Kelly-Irving, epidemiologist

At 11 p.m. on October 12, 1974, a young Stanford University student named Bruce Perry, had an argument with his wife Arlis.[2] The spat was about the tire pressure in their car, and Arlis, a devout young woman, grew upset. She went to pray at the Memorial Church on campus.

She never made it home. At 3 a.m. Bruce called the Stanford police to report his wife missing. The police checked the church and found all the doors locked. The next morning, however, Arlis Perry's body was found inside. She was the victim of a grisly, ritual murder.

There were three possible suspects: an unknown random attacker, the campus night watchman, and Bruce Perry. No evidence at the scene matched the watchman or Perry, and a polygraph later ruled out Perry as a suspect.

For 43 years, it was the most famous unsolved murder in Santa Clara County, California. Then, in 2018, a scrap of DNA from the scene gave police enough evidence to get a search warrant for the night watchman's apartment. When deputies arrived to serve the warrant, the suspect shot himself in the head.

We don't know how this experience fashioned Perry's career, but it seems apparent that it must have, because trauma became Bruce Perry's specialty.

Perry continued his studies at Stanford, eventually concentrating in psychiatry and neuroscience. He has worked with survivors of the Branch Davidian siege in Waco, Texas, survivors of the Oklahoma City bombing, and survivors of the Columbine and Sandy Hook school shootings.

As Perry explains in *The Boy Who Was Raised As a Dog*, "I have made it my life's work to understand how trauma affects children and to develop innovative ways to help them cope with it."[3]

Bruce Perry's Model of the Nervous System

Bruce Perry's experiences led him to develop a therapeutic model based on the levels of the brain.[4] From our newest and most sophisticated brain level down to our oldest and most primitive level, the brain looks like this:

- Cortex

- Limbic Brain

- Diencephalon

- Brainstem

These four regions are interconnected.

The brainstem connects the brain and spinal cord, and the diencephalon resides at the base of the brain. Together these two regulate basic processes like breathing, heartrate, vision, hearing, and the sleep and wake cycles.[5]

The limbic system is buried under the cortex and regulates emotion and memory, and how we relate to others. The newest part of the brain, the cortex, sits atop the brain. It regulates voluntary actions, reasoning, and thought.

To reach the thinking part of the brain, a message has to travel from the lower two regions to the upper two regions. But when a child has been subjected to trauma or high stress levels, the lower levels of the brain can short-circuit the incoming message.

As Bruce Perry observes, the lower levels of the brain cannot tell time and they cannot think.[6] Consequently, as new information comes in, the lower portions of the brain may trigger a response that dates from an older period of time. The time trauma occurred.

When that happens the person acts automatically, without thinking, and in a way out of touch with the present situation.

Once the lower brain areas have become dysregulated—a common effect of abuse and neglect—they can produce responses that interfere with the person's relationships and reasoning. That's why early experiences are so critical. As Perry says, "...the developing brain is exquisitely sensitive to stress."[7]

Another way of saying this is that the past keeps appearing as if it is present.

As we suggested in an earlier chapter, just as workmen use scaffolding to build a building, a child needs their parents to provide the emotional, social, and intellectual scaffolding they need to develop in healthy ways.[8] When the parents fail to provide effective scaffolding, it leads to chronic dysregulation in the child.[9]

That's why changing habits—which are actually neural networks—is a process the child of an alcoholic must undergo. But how do you get the voice of a belittling parent out of your head? How do you get the indifference of a neglectful parent out of your head? How do you get the ruminations of a drunk out of your head? That's the problem.

If you don't figure out a solution, your habitual ways of thinking and acting will grow stronger and block your ability to be successful in one area, multiple areas, or in all areas of your life.

The old habits will block your ability to be at peace with yourself, even when you are alone.

That's why the child of an alcoholic needs to realize that some patterns, formed as a reaction to the alcoholic and enabler, are harmful. But by the time that is realized, the neural pathways may have become as fixed as railroad tracks.

As an adult, you may think...

- I am a people-pleaser, but that destroys my sense of self, so I won't do it.
- I am afraid of authority, but I no longer need to fear authority, so I won't do it.

- I judge myself harshly, but negative self-talk hurts me, so I won't do it.
- And so on...

You can go down the whole list of things you want to change about yourself and say, "I won't do that anymore," and it won't make a dent in your behavior. Bruce Perry's view of the nervous system explains why.

But there is a different way to look at the nervous system. It is the subject of the next chapter.

Chapter 12

The Nervous System, Part 2

> "The state that saved them was a state
> from which they could not easily get out of."
> —Steven Porges, neuroscientist

In her book *Anchored*, therapist Deb Dana offers a threefold way of thinking about the human nervous system.[1]

About 500 million years ago, there lived a class of fish, the *placoderm*. We know them only from their fossils, and they matter for only one reason. We share a feature of our nervous system with them.

The placoderm could shut down, go numb, or enter a state of collapse—the emotional equivalent of a turtle retreating into its shell.

Roughly 400 million years ago, another class of fish appeared. Again, we know them only from their fossils. This group was the *acanthodian*. These fish could defend themselves through action, or what we know as fight-or-flight. We share this feature of our nervous system with them.

Finally, 200 million years ago, a nervous system characteristic emerged that is unique to mammals. It is a calming state, and it allows us to connect with other people.

Three Pathways of Response

We inherited all three pathways of response from our very distant relatives.[2] Each ensures our safety, though in different ways or at different times. The oldest way says, hide. The second oldest way says, act. The newest way says, calm yourself through connecting with others and engaging in social relationships.

This way of thinking about the nervous system is part of Polyvagal Theory, the brainchild of a behavioral neuroscientist named Steven Porges. Porges' primary interest was in the way the nervous system develops in newborns.

Porges admits, at the time he did his research, he had no idea his theory could shed light on how people respond to trauma. But even before he published *The Polyvagal Theory* in 2011, therapists had seized on his ideas as an explanation for what they observed in clients.

Wayne once knew two Vietnam veterans, Ed and Dan.

Ed was a Marine who had seen intense combat. When Wayne ran into him, he never knew what to expect. Ed might say hello, or equally likely, he might not answer Wayne, as if Wayne were invisible. When Ed didn't answer, he didn't appear to see Wayne either.

Ed illustrates the oldest part of our nervous system. He was numb and largely shut down, and he seemed consumed by some interior drama.

Dan was an airborne military policeman in Vietnam. Dan illustrates the second oldest state of our nervous system—action (fight or flight). Though Dan was not in direct combat, he constantly had to evaluate situations for danger. Even after leaving the war zone, scanning for danger became a habit he could not shake.

Neither Dan nor Ed could overcome the state they were in. And neither Dan nor Ed could get into the most desirable state—the state of calm engagement with the world and other people.

As the child of an alcoholic and enabler, you also may struggle to reach the state of calm engagement with the world and other people.

If that's the case, you could adopt Bruce Perry's point of view, and see that the lower part of your brain is interfering with messages trying to reach your cortex. Or you could adopt Steven Porges' point of view, and see yourself as stuck in one of two primitive ways of dealing with the world.

But whichever view you adopt, it doesn't matter because both point to the need to recalibrate your nervous system. That's why we will soon discuss recalibration. But before we go there, we must mention something else.

Chapter 13

Shame

> "For years a secret shame destroyed my peace"
> —Justin Richardson, British poet

My life has been a disaster. My father was a legendary drunk who lied, chased women, and left us penniless when he died at age 48. My mother was hooked on prescription pills, smoked like a chimney, and was miserable until she passed. My sister is alcoholic and will probably die drunk.

I managed to get a master's degree and some successes, but typically in relationships I lose myself and the rest of my life crashes and burns. I've been so codependent in the past I lost a job by trying to please a woman. Then, of course, she left because I didn't have a job! I suppose I have to laugh about that.

I had some problems with booze also, but I haven't drunk in 12 years. Here is something you wrote which definitely applies to me: "The effects on children of living with an alcoholic are well known. These include depression, inability to form close relationships, relentless self-criticism, inability to complete projects, and constant approval seeking. Children growing up in a household with an alcoholic are damaged children."

I am resilient and keep going, trying to live a spiritual life, but sometimes feel like giving up. I married a beautiful but materialistic woman who committed adultery with a wealthy man, stole my money, and left after she put a curse on me with a chicken egg. No, I'm not kidding.

I obviously made a bad decision. I didn't drink a drop through all this, but now I have little hope for the future. It could be a lot worse. I have little money, but at least I have no alimony or child support payments. I am physically healthy, and I have a good job.

My question is: what hope is there for us damaged folk? I've made a ton of progress from where I was 20 years ago, but I am afraid to do anything now lest some unknown character defect, caused by my childhood, ambush my thinking and cause me more pain in the future. I have become the poster boy for caution.

Clint

Clint's question—What hope is there for us damaged folk?—is the question that hangs over this book and each of the following chapters.

Understanding Shame

The feeling of being damaged goods has a name. Shame.[1]

A baby, a toddler, and a child see themselves reflected in their parents' eyes. When a parent traffics in abuse and neglect, the child often sees themselves as worthy of abuse and neglect. The child might then break contact with their fledgling self and internalize how the parent sees them.

This is true, even though it has nothing to do with who the child is or can be.

Shame is a feeling of chronic worthlessness, and it includes at least three sub-beliefs.

- There is something inherently wrong with me.
- I will be found out for the worthless person I am.
- Things will never get better.

These feelings can be overwhelming, but the child lacks the maturity to understand where they came from. As a consequence, children of alcoholics often feel shame over the smallest mistakes.

The core fear of our youngest selves is abandonment, and abandonment is the underlying element behind shame. We fear no one will take our side, and somehow, it is our fault.

This fear, and the shame it generates, develop a merciless inner critic in children of alcoholics. The inner critic tells them to be extremely hard on themselves, and nothing they can do will ever be good enough, because they are inherently unworthy.

Since the feeling lacks details, the child of an alcoholic doesn't understand where it comes from. The result? They end up stuck with shame-based thoughts which sap their energy and lead to more isolation and self-hatred.

In detail, this is what it can be like.

A thought or sensation will blitzkrieg through the child of an alcoholic's mind for a microsecond. It might be a fearful voice they hear or the sight of a traumatic image. But the sensation disappears before the conscious mind can register it, and it plunges the child of an alcoholic into crippling behavior they cannot control.

So the child of an alcoholic grows up ashamed of themselves and ashamed of the secrets they carry. However, once they are free of these feelings, the child of an alcoholic realizes shame only when they fail to live up to their own values. That is the normal role of shame in life.

Flipping the Shame Script

One man told us he was able to blunt his shame by flipping the script. In a thundering voice, he would recite all the words a thesaurus uses to describe alcoholics:

Drunk, drunkard, intoxicated, inebriate, wino, boozer, souse, loaded, tipsy, wasted, lush, plastered, hammered, rummy, sloshed, bombed, tippler, dipsomaniac, tanked, sot, besotted, juiced, stewed, boozy, sozzled, blotto, under the influence, crapulous, blitzed, crocked, bender, binge, imbiber, befuddled.

At least for the moment, it calmed his shame. He told us he only regretted he couldn't find a comparable list for enablers.

This man did not excuse his parents for what they did, when he was right before their eyes on a daily basis. He did not excuse them, he said, because people with only a tiny window into his life saw something was radically wrong. Occasionally, a neighbor or kindly teacher would reach out to him, but they didn't know what to say, and he didn't know how to ask for help.

If you, the reader, decide not to seek help, it is most likely shame that is holding you back. That, in itself, shows that you need the help you are afraid to ask for.

Shame was the last item on the list we needed to discuss before raising the most obvious question of all. What should I do now?

Chapter 14

Recalibration, An Overview

> "There is no prize for the best victim."
> —Chrisjen Avasarala, *The Expanse*

When albatross fly over the deep ocean, they sometimes hit a barren spot where there are no fish. When that happens, they don't waste time searching the same spot over and over. Instead, they fly to an entirely new region.[1]

If you were raised in an alcoholic household, you may have repeatedly tried the same ways of coping. Perhaps you tried talking your mother and father out of their behavior, journaled your feelings, or repeated affirmations. Perhaps you tried prayer.

In our daily lives, we normally stick pretty close to what we know. But when the solutions we can think of don't work, it is time to try something else.

That can be scary because it pushes us into new territory. But venturing into new territory holds the promise of the greatest reward.

Phases of Recovery

Recovery takes time and it has phases, like chapters in a book.

The first phase is about reaching safety and stability. Safety means reducing the amount of your overwhelm. It involves minimizing the effects of unsafe people and places.

The second phase of recovery is about regulating the emotions. As a maltreated child, your emotional set points were overwritten by the environment in which you found yourself. Now those set points need to be recalibrated within the normal range.

Phase three of recovery is about allowing your new self to emerge. For that to happen you must:

- say yes to the quest

- believe in your own potential

- keep knocking at the door

- not stay in a bucket of crabs

That last idea may sound odd, but let us explain. Edward Wilson, who offers outpatient treatment for alcoholics, makes this comparison.[2]

On Kodiak Island, when people pull crabs out of traps, they put them in buckets without lids. They do this for a simple reason. When one crab tries to escape, the other crabs will pull it back down. And Wilson says, "Most so-called alcohol support groups are, in fact, merely a bucket of crabs that will keep dragging you back down to their level."

That's not what you want. You want to escape from the bad things that happened to you.

We don't know where you are in life right now, but we have a few suggestions.

If you are preoccupied with thoughts of harming yourself, you must call a counselor or suicide hotline for help.

If you are not considering hurting yourself, there are other things you can do.

Every child of an alcoholic can benefit from reading about the effects of abuse and neglect. The best place to begin is with books and articles from mental health experts. We have gathered some good books in the Resources page, but there are many other good books. Do an internet search and pick books which speak to you.

You might find helpful books under topics like toxic parents, child abuse, or adult children of alcoholics. Many of the books in the latter category, however, are outdated or not child-centered. Some are even a defense of alcoholics and enablers.

Professional Help

Reading, while helpful, is not enough for one simple reason. We cannot accurately assess ourselves and our own situation.

If you have read our advice column, you know we don't willy-nilly suggest therapy as a solution, because lots of problems in life are not psychological. But being the child of an alcoholic creates genuine psychological problems.

Therapists and psychiatrists are the experts in this area. If you don't know where to begin or who to call, consider the list below and decide who you might approach, based on their field of expertise.

— Depression
— Anxiety and Fear
— Complex PTSD
— Developmental trauma
— Relational trauma
— Attachment disorder
— Dissociation
— Borderline Personality disorder
— Sexual trauma
— PTSD

We listed depression and anxiety separately, though they largely overlap. A simplified way of looking at these two is:
- stress is a response to threats
- anxiety is a response to stress
- depression is a response to unmanaged stress and anxiety.

The Therapy Experience

When a young child falls down, they go to their mother for comfort. If their mother comforts them, they experience her nervous system shifting their own nervous system to a feeling of safety.

Psychotherapy is like that. In therapy, the nervous system of the therapist communicates safety to the nervous system of the client. Once you feel safe, you can open up and honestly reveal your trials.

If you feel embarrassed or ashamed asking for help—something especially common with men—sneak up on it. When you call for help, say you have a problem with depression or anxiety. Those are generic complaints and benign admissions to make.

If you are still unsure where to start, try calling the office of a child psychiatrist or a therapist dealing with trauma in children, and ask for a referral to someone who sees adults. Unless your method of coping has led to substance abuse, you do not need someone in the field of chemical dependency.

Therapy can be expensive. If you have good health insurance or ample financial means, you can begin immediately. If finances are an issue, look for therapists working on a sliding scale, those who do group work, and those who work online.

And if you are still afraid to admit you need help, ease into the problem with one of the many mental health self-help workbooks available. But don't stop there.

Your growth and your life are not in opposition. They are part of one process called your life. You had an adverse childhood experience growing up with an alcoholic, and there were probably more adverse childhood experiences in your home as well.

Growth is what you seek, and growth is the opposite of letting adverse childhood experiences define you.

Focusing on Gains

Dan Sullivan is an executive coach. He often sees people who are unhappy because they have one bad habit: they measure themselves against an ideal of success.[3]

Sullivan tells these people that they cannot be happy until they focus on the gains they make, rather than the gap they feel from some ideal future state.

If you got the dishes done today, when before you let them pile up in the sink, celebrate that. In short, always celebrate your gains, no matter how small, not how far you are from hypothetical perfection.

This chapter has been a brief call to look at your life realistically. In the next chapter we delve into the nitty gritty of doing that. But please remember these facts about children of alcoholics:
- the earlier the damage, the worse the effects
- the longer the damage, the worse the effects

So cut yourself some slack and begin to heal.

Chapter 15

Asking For Help

> If you bring forth what is within you,
> what you bring forth will save you.
> If you do not bring forth what is within you,
> what you do not bring forth will destroy you.
> —Gospel of Thomas, Saying 70

Don't be that person who would die before they opened their mouth and told the truth about their life as the child of an alcoholic.

In telling, you won't be revealing family secrets. You will be stating facts, and you have an absolute right to state the facts about your life.

Wayne's Experience

Wayne learned about the need to ask for help from an experience that almost cost him his life:

I was on my second ship in the Navy, and it was the first time I had been to sea as a navigator. We left San Diego, our home port, and our first stop was Hawaii.

At the time, only the largest navy ships carried satellite navigation, so my tools were crude by today's standards: a sextant, a radar screen, and a seasoned helper.

Making a landfall is a challenge.

For a time, the radar picture grows murkier. Shapes emerge and they don't look like anything on the chart. Navigation, in those days, was like putting together a jigsaw puzzle while driving a car. As you struggle to match pieces, the car hurtles forward.

If you were raised by an alcoholic and an enabler, making sense of your life is like making a landfall. You pick up scraps of information here and there, but for a while, often years or decades, you cannot make sense of it.

First light gave way to sunrise. We steamed past Diamond Head and saw 50 or 60 ships and small boats lying between us and our berth. Cautiously, we threaded our way into Pearl Harbor, and by midmorning our mooring lines were fast to the pier.

This was to be my only day ashore in Hawaii, and I wanted to make the most of it. Because I was on the bridge all night, I missed breakfast. One of the stewards offered to fix me something, but I declined. I didn't want to waste a moment.

With another ship's officer, I rented a car and drove east on the Kalanianaole Highway to Makapu'u Point.

The beach at Makapu'u is one of the best anywhere for bodysurfing. But the beach at Makapu'u Point is also known for riptides and undertow. During much of the year, the current flowing out to sea is rated 'extremely dangerous.'

After half an hour in the water, my companion, exhausted by the surf, went back to where we left our towels. I was tired, too, but nowhere near ready to quit.

What I didn't notice was that each succeeding wave shoved me farther down the coast, until I was approaching rocks at one end of the beach. There an invisible rip current rushed to the sea.

It was then I realized I was being pulled into the Pacific Ocean.

I stopped swimming and felt for the bottom with a toe. It wasn't there.

Exhausted from a night with no sleep and a day without food, I struggled against the current without getting anywhere. Fifty yards away a lifeguard looked the other way. I could have yelled for help, but I didn't. I could have held up my hand in the universal sign of swimmer's distress, but I didn't. Instead, I strained harder against the ocean.

Floundering against the current brought me closer to the rocks and gave me an object to use to measure my progress. I wasn't gaining on the shore, but I could see each stroke drew me slightly closer to the rocks.

I knew I couldn't make the beach, but perhaps, I thought, I could fight my way to the rocks before being swept out to sea.

My eyes were bleary from seawater, but I wasn't giving up. I battled and battled and grew closer to the rocks. At one point, I thrust myself down to touch the seabed. Perhaps, I thought, I could push off the bottom and gain momentum toward the rocks.

That's when the balls of my feet touched solid sand, and I realized the water closest to the rocks was chest high. I was too fatigued to swim, but I thought I had just enough strength to walk ashore against the current. And that's what I did.

Thirty feet away, a lifeguard watched me from the rocks. I hadn't seen him approach. When my eyes met his, neither of us spoke. Fifty feet behind him was a second lifeguard. In silence they watched me wade past. They followed me until I dropped on the beach and fell asleep.

I woke with one thought. I would die before I would ask anyone for help. I never knew that about myself because I was such an outsider to myself.

If you are the child of an alcoholic, chances are you are also an outsider to yourself.

I never told my companion what happened because that's what children of alcoholics do. They are very good at keeping secrets. They have been trained to keep secrets for a long time.

In the previous chapter we mentioned that, while reading is helpful, you cannot self-diagnose. You are too close to yourself to know the wisest thing to do. That's why you should seek external help.

What to Expect

What should you expect from psychological help?

Most importantly, you should expect it to be transformational. While a back rub is nice, the effects are only temporary. Genuine psychological help, however, is more like having a plaster cast removed from your mind.

In your first phone call or in-person meeting, an opening question might go something like, What brings you to therapy? What do you hope to gain from therapy? How are you feeling today?

Even before the first visit you may be asked to fill out some questionnaires. A good therapist knows it took bravery to make the call, and they use questionnaires to know where to begin.

You may feel reluctant to reveal your deepest secrets to a stranger, but chances are your therapist has already heard those secrets. Therapists are typically empathetic, because most of them come from a trauma background themselves.

In therapy, you can be yourself, no matter how little you think of yourself or how dark you think your secrets are. The social taboos about what you can and cannot discuss with other people will fade away as you talk with your therapist.

From those conversations, the therapist learns who you would like to be. As you talk, they may type notes into a computer. What you say won't be revealed to others unless you pose an imminent threat of harm to yourself or others.

Don't be held back by embarrassment or by feeling stupid, backward, and hopeless. Those are common feelings.

You may also be prescribed medication. Some of these meds can change your mood, reduce your anxiety, or clear up mind fog. They may also aid executive functioning—giving you better ability to plan and schedule your daily routine.

From visit to visit you will fill out a mood scale, to see if you are improving.

If you go to a small practice, one person may do all the intake, and they may be the one to decide where to begin treatment.

If you go to a mental health facility or a mental health unit attached to a hospital, you may be screened by a nurse who will compile your medical history, and perhaps measure your height, weight, and blood pressure.

From there you may go to a physician's assistant or nurse practitioner who will ask more questions and evaluate you for possible medications. That sets the stage for therapy to begin.

Once your therapist has made a psychological assessment, the next step is a treatment plan.

In the beginning, the plan may be somewhat hazy, but it will give you a general direction to follow. Good therapists don't want you to stay in therapy. They want you to recover and go on your way, coming back only occasionally if you feel the need.

A good therapist wants to make space for the next person who needs their help.

If the first therapist doesn't help, go to a second or a third until you find someone you have confidence in.

If you reach out and don't find help, or you feel you cannot afford it, that is not an excuse to put this issue on the back burner for another five or 10 years. That would be tragic. You must act now because ruminating on your problems goes nowhere.

Chapter 16

Boundaries

> Dogs may bark, but the caravan moves on.
> —Arabic proverb

Growing up you may have been taught that good people stay close to their family. What you weren't taught is that children from some alcoholic families must jettison one, several, or all the members of their biological family, for the sake of their own well-being.

One of the first things a lifeguard learns is not to let the drowning person drown them, because losing two lives helps no one. In the same way, the first rule for the child of an alcoholic must be Save Yourself.

Boundaries Defined

Many of us have heard about setting boundaries, but what is a boundary?

A boundary is a psychological line in the sand. It is a mental line that separates what is permitted in our presence from what is not. The point of a boundary is simple: to preserve our integrity rather than allowing someone else to run roughshod over us.

Who throws you off balance? Who causes you to be upset? Those are the people whose influence needs to be curtailed, perhaps for now, perhaps forever.

We are not saying imposing boundaries on others, even family, is your ideal first choice. We are saying it is often the necessary choice, if you want to heal. The longer you engage with people who don't have your best interest at heart, the more likely you will do something you regret.

Child welfare advocate Andrew Vachss put the matter clearly when he said, "Family should be an operational term, not a biological term."[1] What he meant was, a man is your father because he acts like a father, not because he donated sperm. In the same way, a woman is your mother because she acts like your mother, not because she donated an egg.

For people who grew up in maltreatment, the only way to save themselves and have a decent life may be to walk away. That sounds cold, but for many it is essential.

As a child, you had no choice but to run down the neurological pathways that were established as you grew up. Your task now is creating new, healthy neurological pathways until they become your deeply ingrained, automatic, default settings. To do that, you may need to set boundaries in your life.

In practice, what does that mean? Let's look at a few scenarios.

A woman writes...

My alcoholic brother will not apologize for his horrendous behavior at our son's wedding last October. In the past I would try nicely and ask him to cut back on his drinking when he visited. Our furniture wasn't so lucky. He would break our chairs when he plopped down.

At our son's wedding he showed up in dirty torn clothes though I offered to buy him a suit. He drank before he arrived, even after I asked him to please not drink that day. The moment my back was turned at the reception, he went to the microphone after I asked him not to.

I thought for one split second he might say something heartwarming. All he said was, "Get a divorce, sell the house, go to Vegas." Then he sat down laughing, tossing the gift my son and daughter-in-law made for all the guests up into the air like a ball.

I was so mortified. My husband was in shock. We did not want to make a scene and cause further embarrassment, but a family friend asked him to please be respectful of his nephew and the bride. Shortly after, he left, thank goodness.

For several weeks he called and left messages on our phone saying how great it was to be part of the wedding and reception. He also asked for an invitation to our home at Christmas. I was so angry I did not return his calls until December 27th.

With as much compassion as possible I told him why he was not invited to spend Christmas with my family. I said my sons do not want to be around him anymore. I said what he did at the wedding was so humiliating he will not be invited to my youngest son's wedding.

I have always been there for him when the rest of the family turned their backs due to the way he treats them. When his apartment burnt down, I bought him all new clothes, toiletries, coats and shoes when my other siblings would not even give him $20.

I love my brother, and it fills my heart with such sadness not to include him in my life, but I have had enough. He will never acknowledge the hurt he causes me or apologize.

Should he and other estranged relatives be invited to events because of right or entitlement, or should invitations to a bridal shower, wedding or christening be a privilege?

Lena

Lena, let's talk about your brother first and assume the disease model of alcoholism is correct.

Your brother has a disease. But what kind of disease? Self-contained, or infectious? Obviously it is infectious. His disease ruins once-in-a-lifetime events like a wedding and recurring events like Christmas.

Infectious diseases must be quarantined.

He also suffers from alcoholic vanity. He thinks he is the cleverest dog in the pack while making a spectacle of himself.

His comments at your son's wedding reveal how distorted his thinking is. Getting involved with him in tit-for-tat discussions will do nothing but frustrate you. You can't reason with a drunk. What you can do is, once and for all, let him know your door will be open to him if he changes. Then end contact.

Of course it fills your heart with sadness, because family ties are wired into our memories and into our DNA. But sometimes behavior trumps biology, and this is one of those times.

But what about other estranged relatives? You seem such a kind and open person we can't imagine you are at the root of any of this. So we suggest following two rules.

First, closeness. Invite only those you are close to. Second, feedback. Invite only those who give you positive feedback.

Don't let ideas of 'should' and 'ought' rule your behavior. Let the reality of others' behavior be your guide, not ideas of right, entitlement or privilege.

Wayne & Tamara

Another woman writes...

I just separated from my husband this weekend, and my heart literally feels torn from my inside. But I asked for it. We've only been married a year. We dated two years prior to that, and I fell for him mostly because he is The Man of all men.

He is so precious, but I took advantage of that. We clicked so well. I started having family problems with my father and brothers who are alcoholics, and I wanted to be there for them, a little too much. I ran up there constantly (they live six hours away), and I made plans to have one of my brothers move in with me to get him out of a bad situation.

My husband disagreed. Ever since, there grew a distance between us. I started seeing someone else, never sexually, but it was still cheating. A few months ago I told my husband, and he begged me to work on our marriage. So we went to counseling.

A few weeks ago I started to feel our marriage was a mistake, so I brought up my feelings. He apparently had enough of hearing it and took all necessary steps to arrange our divorce. I guess that's why I'm writing.

Not only do you now know how much of a loser I am, but also that I realize giving him up is one of the hardest things I've ever had to do. Let me tell you, I've faced guns put to family members' heads as a child and that was a piece of cake compared to this experience.

I bawled and felt empty all weekend. It's Sunday night and I'm about to lose it, but before I do, I want to ask you one thing. Would it be a mistake to move up north away from it all to be with my family, or would it be wise?

Judging from what I've told you about my family I think I know the answer. I just need to hear it from some people who know their stuff.
Remi

Remi, your father had a disorder. It might be his fault. It might be someone else's fault. It might be in his DNA. It might be a disease. It might be the result of converging factors. We don't care what the explanation is.

His disorder was communicable. He infected your brothers with his disorder, and he also infected you. How deep was his infection? This deep.

Human beings have an inborn bias in favor of protecting the young. But your father was so deeply infected he couldn't or wouldn't stop drinking, though the disastrous results on his children were right before his eyes.

Now you wonder if going back to the cause of your life's problems is the answer. That idea makes no sense. It shows how deeply you have been infected…

Guidelines for Setting Boundaries

If you don't know, in advance, what your boundaries are and why they are there, you will cave under pressure.

Here are a few guidelines for setting boundaries.
- identify your limits
- be specific and clear on what your boundaries are
- communicate your boundaries clearly
- be willing to enforce your boundaries
- be consistent in enforcing your boundaries
- expect the process to make you uncomfortable, especially in the beginning

Consider this letter about setting boundaries…

I am writing during a trying time in my life. I am a 35-year-old mother of three children and just recently lost my husband. My siblings and I have been dealing with an alcoholic mother since we were born. There were harsh and horrible memories, but I believe we have all forgiven her.

My father who did not drink, but worked two full-time jobs, divorced her when the youngest of us kids was a teenager. My mother has gone through ups and downs ever since. Two years ago she was arrested again for drunk driving. After realizing she'd be facing prison time, she attempted suicide many times.

The worst time my mother landed in intensive care for a week on a respirator, unconscious, while her children, sister and brother sat vigil by her bedside. We were told if paramedics arrived 10 minutes later she would have died. Each time she attempted to kill herself, she called one of us kids to let us know and say goodbye after taking all the pills.

Well, she ended up doing the time assigned by the court and came out at first a calm and happy person, but she wasn't given her old job back. She has a fear of working in public, so she won't take a cashiering job close enough to walk to. As a result she is about to be evicted from her apartment.

Since I lost my husband, who was also an alcoholic, I've found a cheaper apartment for myself and my children. It has an extra bedroom I'd like to use as a playroom. My uncle offered my mother a place to stay, but she says she doesn't like his rules.

She is demanding to move in with me. She still drinks and has mood swings that explode at the drop of a hat. I don't believe it would be good for my children so I told her no. I told her to stay with her brother. She told me not to consider her my mother anymore. Her last words were, "I'll never hate you, but I'll never speak to you again."

I feel guilty, but I also know my children come first. They are still dealing with their father's death, as it happened just four months ago. I feel hurt and angry my mother cannot understand what she is doing to me at such a painful point in my family's life.

Marti

Marti, you cannot comprehend why a drunken woman doesn't understand what she is doing to your family. For people not raised in an alcoholic household that is not even a question. They would be astonished if your mother didn't attempt to destroy your family's life.

When you were young, your mother prepared a cocktail for you and your siblings. She mixed normal with what is normal only in alcoholic households. One result is you can say "I married an alcoholic" as casually as another woman might say, "I was raised Lutheran, so I married a Lutheran."

Every aspect of your life, and now it appears your children's lives, has been affected by alcohol. You say your kids come first. That's only believable if you eliminate alcoholism from their home life. That you feel guilty about not bringing your mother into your home suggests you haven't grasped the full extent of her abuse.

Legal and medical professionals who deal with people like your mother couldn't help her. You can't either. But you can get professional help to grow past the trauma you were raised in. The last thing you want to do is replicate the horror of your childhood for your children.

Living under your uncle's rules may be the last chance your mother gets to put her life in order. Her life suggests families need to move away from saving the drunkard to saving the six or 16 lives around the drunkard which are being mutilated.

Wayne & Tamara

As we told one woman about giving into the demands from her alcoholic father, you can't let a door-to-door salesman talk on and on. If he's selling something you don't want, you close the door. That's what setting a boundary means.

In the last three chapters, we suggested opening yourself up to therapy and setting boundaries. It all sounds so overwhelming. How do you create breathing room for yourself? We have two suggestions in the next chapter.

Chapter 17

Understanding Yourself

> "A schedule defends from chaos and whim.
> It is a net for catching days."
> —Annie Dillard, writer

Many children of alcoholics are masters at doing last things first and first things not at all. If that applies to you, you need to set up simple routines and practices to order your day.

Suggestion One: Put Order In Your Day

Having a ritual for starting and ending the day is a good way to begin. You might start each day with a calming and centering routine, meditating, or repeating the goals which are most important to you. You can end the day in the same way.

If you are unaccustomed to establishing a routine, this will be hard. That's why you don't want to take on too much too soon.

One famous study found that creating a simple habit, like eating a piece of fruit with breakfast, took people an average of 66 days to establish.[1] Some, however, took as long as 254 days to establish the same habit. That same research found that exercise habits can take 50 percent longer to establish than the fruit habit.

It may take even more time for you to feel the rewards of a new routine.

That is not, however, a reason to be discouraged. Research shows that sporadic failures don't necessarily increase the amount of time needed to establish a habit.

When you fail or forget today, begin again tomorrow. As many spiritual traditions say, no effort on the right path is ever lost.

If you have a problem establishing a daily routine, these habits are worth considering:
- use a daily planner
- write things down
- track your time
- schedule a regular time for organizing your day, week, or month

This kind of planning can seem overwhelming. That's why we suggest a method from Randy Ingermanson, a computational physicist and novelist.[2]

He suggests handling overwhelm this way:
- write down everything you think you need to do
- list things small enough to do today
- list things small enough to do this week
- give yourself permission to do everything else some other time.
- begin each day with a short to-do list culled from your weekly list
- make each daily list small and achievable
- when you accomplish today's things, you are done
- tomorrow, do the same thing

The overall rule is, minimize the commotion in your life until you are strong enough to stand up for yourself and follow your own inner compass. Because everything we allow in our life affects our well-being.

Suggestion Two: Persist, Even When Progress Seems Slow

Changing your life is hard. When you fail, you will feel as if you are being thrown back to the very beginning, with no progress to show for your effort. But that isn't true.

It's more like this.

We had a friend named George. George was doing graduate work at the University of Iowa, which is in Iowa City.

George and his wife drove to Chicago one weekend to visit family. On the way back, it began to snow. When they reached Davenport, Iowa, they were 60 miles from Iowa City, and they had to slow down to 60 miles per hour because of the snow.

That meant they were an hour from home.

When they were 30 miles from Iowa City, it began snowing harder. They had to reduce their speed to 30 miles per hour. That meant they were still an hour away from home.

The snow continued until it was almost a whiteout. At that point, they were 10 miles from Iowa City and could only drive 10 miles an hour. They were still an hour away from home.

That's what change can feel like. Even though you are making progress, often great progress, you can't see it. It feels like you are forever an hour away from the destination.

Did George and his wife arrive home? Of course. In the same way, you will arrive at your destination if you persist. Just find a place to begin.

Spend Your Energy on Healing

Before we leave this chapter, there is one other matter to mention.

Some children of alcoholics would like to give their parents a piece of their mind. That's what the following letter writer had in mind.

I am 30, married, with two daughters. I am now discovering the effects my alcoholic parents had on me. I am in college studying for a bachelor's degree in human services, and I have learned a lot about what I went through as a child.

So, I confronted my mother about her addiction. On the phone she ignores my words and hangs up on me. When I emailed, she replied she no longer considers herself my mother. I know I cannot change her, she can only change herself. But I want her to know how she's impacted me.

I also want her not to act the fool when the children or I visit. She strips naked, uses vulgar language, et cetera. I haven't heard from her in a month.

I do not know what to do. Do I stay away and wait for her to realize what she is missing?

Lana

Lana, saying alcoholism is a disease is only partly correct. Alcoholism is an infectious disease. It spreads its effects on everyone who comes in contact with the alcoholic.

Normally the ones most damaged are family members, especially children in the home of the alcoholic, because alcoholism is also child abuse. However, the infection often spreads to strangers, as when an alcoholic maims or kills another with an automobile.

Active alcoholics are smug because they live in a world of imagination where they make the rules. They believe the real world must pay homage to them because they refuse to pay homage to the real world. Quarantine is often the only effective way to deal with this infectious disease.

Your mother will not acknowledge her failings because that is the first step toward sobriety, and what she cares most about is drinking. Your mother will not acknowledge her faults because that is the first step in admitting she neglected you. Why would she admit her negative impact on your life? There is nothing in it for her.

If you lost the use of a hand in an accident, you could forever lament what happened, or you could go forward and live your life to the fullest. In the same way, the accident of your birth destroyed the inborn hopes you have for your family. All you can do is accept that reality and move forward.

You are not responsible for your mother's actions, and you should not look on this as some great family secret. When asked by friends why you don't go to see your mother, be forthright in your explanation. Tell them she is carrying a disease and you need to protect yourself and your children from that disease.

Wayne & Tamara

In general, expecting an alcoholic or an enabler to recognize how they harmed you is a waste of time. Your energy is better spent healing yourself.

We've said a lot about you as the child of an alcoholic. In the next three chapters, we'll turn our attention to alcoholics and enablers.

Chapter 18

Alcoholics Anonymous

> "If you want to be an expert, invent the territory."
> —John Lilly, psychoanalyst, inventor

The territory of alcoholism didn't exist until two blackout drunks, Bill Wilson and Bob Smith, met. Wilson was a down-and-out stockbroker and Smith a proctologist.

Their collaboration began on June 10, 1935, when Bob Smith took his last drink.[1] That date is considered the founding day of Alcoholics Anonymous (AA). Three years later, Bill Wilson began writing the bible of AA, called 'the Big Book.' It is the foundation of AA's Twelve Steps.

When Alcoholics Anonymous arrived on the scene in the 1930s, there was little help available to heavy drinkers, and the new organization offered benefits.

AA was:
- free
- open to everyone
- worked for some people
- provided group membership

In 1941, an AA member perusing the New York Herald Tribune ran across a notice in the Memoriam column.[2] It read, "Mother—God grant me the serenity to accept things I cannot change, courage to change things I can, and wisdom to know the difference. Goodbye."

That remembrance was copied, altered, and circulated throughout the Alcoholics Anonymous network. By the late 1940s, it was christened the Serenity Prayer.[3]

In 1960 E. M. Jellinek, a biostatistician, published *The Disease Concept of Alcoholism*.[4] Though the book was based on a tiny sample of self-selected participants, it is "widely considered to be the first scientific typology that was developed into a comprehensive theory of alcoholism as a disease."[5]

Previous views of dipsomania, as it was called, consisted mostly of "armchair observations and poorly organized clinical notes."[6]

The Nature of AA

Bill Wilson and Bob Smith were active members of a fundamentalist, evangelical organization called the Oxford Group. Many practices of that group carried over to Alcoholics Anonymous.[7]

AA's fundamentalist nature is evident in its strict doctrine: alcoholism is a disease and total abstinence is the only cure. That belief echoes the gospel of John, "I am the way, the truth, and the life: no man cometh unto the Father, but by me."[8]

The evangelical element of AA is evident in the last of its Twelve steps: "Having had a spiritual awakening as the result of these steps, we tried to carry this message to alcoholics." That step mirrors Mark the evangelist. "Go ye into all the world, and preach the gospel to every creature."[9]

In heft, AA's Big Book resembles a bible, and like other bibles, it is full of contradictions. For example, while it claims alcoholism is a disease, the idea that it is a moral failing is baked into the Twelve Steps.

Step 4 enjoins alcoholics to make "a searching and fearless moral inventory" of themselves. Step 5 speaks of "the exact nature of our wrongs," and Step 6 implores alcoholics to be "ready to have God remove all these defects of character."

The Disease Concept of Alcoholism

In the 1990s, the disease concept of alcoholism was popularized on the basis that repeated use of the drug changes an alcoholic's brain structure.

But that argument is lame. Everything changes brain structure, from playing the clarinet to learning Dutch. And as we have seen, child abuse and neglect make significant changes in the most vulnerable brains, the brains of children. Does that make abuse and neglect diseases?

Our view is the term *disease* has lost its meaning. It has been used to describe everything from cancer to homelessness. And David Sinclair, one of the foremost experts on aging, considers aging itself to be a disease![10]

The problem with accepting alcoholism as a disease is the word *disease* makes people think of Ebola, tuberculosis, and multiple sclerosis. People see that alcoholism doesn't fit. After all, you can't cure a genuine disease by standing up in a meeting and saying, "My name is Suzanne, and I have breast cancer."

Addiction Defined

The writer Steven Pressfield once defined addiction in the fewest possible words, and he defined it in a way that cuts through all the jargon about Alcohol Use Disorder.[11]

Pressfield said, "All addictions share, among others, two primary qualities. One, they embody repetition without progress. Two, they produce incapacity as a payoff." That is the best concise description of alcoholism we know of.

Addiction specialist Gabor Maté argues that there is one fundamental addiction process, and alcoholism is just an example.[12] Other examples include workaholism, eating disorders, and the use of substances like heroin, nicotine, and cocaine. Some people are addicted to shopping, others to laxatives, and still others to gambling.

While the intent of the disease concept of alcoholism was to reduce the stigma of 'skid row drunks,' it begs a question. Does the stigma arise because the rest of us are uncaring, insensitive louts, or does it arise because drunkenness disgusts us?

Disgust is a primary human emotion, and the nonsensical musings of alcoholics are, frankly, disgusting. So is the stumbling, the gaslighting, the sneaking around.

Psychiatrist Sally Satel and psychologist Scott Lilienfeld once explained why stigmatization can be helpful.[13] "Stigmatization is a normal part of social interaction—a potent force in shaping behavior." (That's why we stigmatize drunk driving.) They add, "There is nothing unethical—and everything natural and socially adaptive—about condemning reckless and harmful acts."

But if you still want to call alcoholism a disease, then classify it as the kind of disease it is.

It is an infectious disease that puts family members and members of society at grave risk. The normal treatment for infectious diseases is quarantine, in order to isolate the carrier and minimize the danger to those without the disease.

To the child of an alcoholic, of course, the alcoholic does not have a disease. They are the disease.

How To View Alcoholics

But if alcoholism is not a disease or a moral failing, how should we look at alcoholics?

Herbert Fingarette, a philosopher at the University of California and consultant to the World Health Organization on alcoholism and addiction, proposed a middle way.[14]

Fingarette said, "If our righteous condemnation is not in order, neither is our cooperation in excusing heavy drinkers or helping them evade responsibility for change."

That is a balanced view, because alcoholics not only kill their own dreams, they often kill their children's dreams as well.

Bridget Grant was an epidemiologist and biometrician at the National Institute of Alcohol Abuse and Alcoholism. Grant and her associates looked at data from over 43,000 adult alcoholics in one study and over 36,000 alcoholics in another.[15] They concluded that, "Treatment rates for AUD remain low (<10%) despite the significant rise in high-risk drinking and AUD..."

The problem with alcoholics and recovery is the story of the funnel and the water. The amount of water you can move through a funnel is determined by the size of the neck, not by the speed of the pouring.

The rate-limiting step with Alcohol Use Disorder is determined by one thing, the person taking authentic steps to end their drinking and drinking-related behavior.

But this is a person who drinks for escape, avoidance, and oblivion. We are talking about someone who will, for years, deny they have a problem. If they ever admit to it, it is likely just another ploy to get someone off their back. That's the bottleneck.

The director of one treatment center told us, "The best way to deny you are an alcoholic is by admitting it."

What he meant was that when an alcoholic finally admits to a drinking problem, it is like a politician's speech. It doesn't mean they believe what they are saying; it means they think it is what someone else wants to hear.

An Australian study found that the median time to first treatment by an alcoholic is 18 years.[16] In the United States, the gap is said to be about 10 years.[17] So, if we assume the average time to first treatment is 10 years, it means a child will spend 3,650 consecutive days dealing with an alcoholic *before* the alcoholic seeks treatment.

This doesn't include the years after initial treatment, when the person falls off the wagon repeatedly. It doesn't include another common problem either. Though the person no longer drinks, their personality may be the same or worse than it was before. That fact is frequently overlooked in statistics on alcoholics.

In 2020 the Cochrane Group, a respected research group, measured success rates among alcoholics.[18] They found results similar to what they found in 2006, with at best minor improvements. In addition, none of the research they examined included information about the alcoholic's quality of life, the family's quality of life, or evidence of a fundamental change in the alcoholic's personality.

Personally, we view alcoholism not as a disease but as an unhealthy adaptation to life.

The problem for children of alcoholics is that the field of alcoholism has been dominated by people whose primary interest is the alcoholic. For people in the field, even the best-intentioned, the alcoholic is the center of their universe. The children have meaning only in reference to the alcoholic.

As a result, little real progress has been made in helping children of alcoholics. Bridget Grant once characterized the alcoholic home as "stressful, chaotic, and frightening."[19] We agree.

This chapter has been about alcoholics. But what about people who choose to stay with an alcoholic? Those people—enablers—are the subject of the next two chapters.

Chapter 19

Enablers And Bonding

> "There is always a pay-off for being the enabler—otherwise what is the point of not developing one's moral integrity?"
> —Anonymous, *My Brave Heart*

A woman writes...
I can't begin to tell you the hopelessness I feel, so I'll spare all details. The summary is I stayed 40 years in an alcoholic marriage, watching helplessly as the environment destroyed my children and turned me into a sickly, fearful woman. I worked, cared for my children, and just kept going.

My husband is now retired, and I help care for my grandchildren while their divorced moms try to pick up the pieces of their own lives. I don't know how to leave. I am so ashamed of my part in this mess. My children will not involve themselves. What can I do?

Catherine

A woman dating a physically abusive, alcoholic man writes, "I had my doubts about our future since the day I met him, but my love is so deep I always convince myself there's no one else for me."

Another woman, the mother of two, married to an alcoholic for 10 years, tells us she believes in "the merit of working things out." But her letter shows absolutely nothing is being worked out or getting better.

A woman in a similar situation writes, "I thank God for bringing him this far." Despite what she says, however, part of her wants to tell the truth.

The letter lists all the ways her husband's behavior is growing worse, and not a single way it is growing better.

A different woman writes, "I am in a marriage with an alcoholic who is in recovery. I deal with lies, broken promises, rage, and denial. You know the profile. My intuition says time, perhaps 15 or 20 years, is needed for some relationships to settle down. What do you think?"

Following that line of wishful thinking, a woman writes, "I can't help but wonder, if he is able to get himself straight, wouldn't it be worth it to move forward together, because we would then have 50-plus years of a healthy relationship?"

Some writers married to alcoholics claim, "He has so much potential," which is another version of "I love him for who I want him to be." Or the writers act as if their children are blind to the impact of heavy drinking, when in fact the children know it to the core of their being.

In the letters we receive, denial in enablers appears as robust as denial in alcoholics.

Two things catch our attention. First, the number of enablers who have the financial means to leave yet don't, and second, the number of people who know they are with an alcoholic but still decide to have children.

Animal Research

This chapter focuses on one question—the traits of enablers. To begin to address that question, we need to turn the clock back 70 years, and talk about something you may not have considered.

In the 1950s and 1960s, Harry Harlow conducted experiments with rhesus monkeys.[1] In one experiment, Harlow separated babies from their mother hours after birth. The infants were placed in wire cages, each with two mother dolls.

One mother doll was wood, covered with sponge rubber and terrycloth. A lightbulb behind her provided warmth. The other mother surrogate was constructed from bare wire and had no lightbulb behind her.

The cloth and wire mothers were placed in compartments alongside the infants' living space.

For half the monkeys, the cloth mother provided milk from a bottle; for half the monkeys, the wire mother provided the milk. The theory at the time was that infants bond to their mother through food.

That proved not to be the case. It didn't matter which mother provided the milk. The infants spent nearly all day clutching the soft, warm surrogate mother, even if she was without milk.

In another experiment, baby monkeys were let loose in an unfamiliar room. If the cloth mother was present, they clutched and touched her, then used her as a base from which to explore the room. But if the cloth mother was absent, these same baby monkeys froze. They crouched, feverishly clutched themselves, and rocked.

When only the wire-mother was present, a different group of monkeys acted like the monkeys who missed their cloth mother. They rocked, crouched in terror, and feverishly clutched at themselves. It was the softness and warmth they craved.

Harry Harlow summarized what he found in a poem he composed.

The Elephant
Though mother may be short on arms,
Her skin is full of warmth and charms,
And mother's touch on baby's skin,
Endears the heart that beats within.

Human Research and Styles of Attachment

In the 1960s and 1970s, studies of human infants yielded comparable results.[2]

The researchers discovered that human children have four different styles of attachment to their main caregiver. They called the styles secure, ambivalent, avoidant, and disorganized.

Why should you care?

Because these four styles of attachment are believed to persist into adulthood and form a template for adult romantic relationships.

Secure Attachment

Secure attachment forms when parents consistently meet the physical and emotional needs of the child.

Securely attached children:
- cry less
- explore more
- do better in school
- are less anxious
- are more mature than the less securely attached
- are more responsive to their parents, and their parents are more responsive to them

As adults, securely attached children enter into longer lasting relationships, have better self-esteem, more independence, and are less prone to depression.

Types of Insecure Attachment

There are three types of insecure attachment: ambivalent, avoidant, and disorganized.[3]

Ambivalently attached children receive inconsistent love and attention from their parents. When separated from their parents, they show distress, yet they are not comforted by the parent's return. They are suspicious of strangers, less confident in exploring the world, and more clingy.

As adults, ambivalently attached people are reluctant to trust others and worry their partner does not love them.

Children with the avoidant attachment style have caregivers who are consistently unresponsive to their needs or emotionally unavailable. As a result, these kids do not go to their parents for comfort and contact. As adults, they have problems with intimacy and are unwilling to share their thoughts and feelings with others.

The fourth attachment style, disorganized, is caused by growing up in fear.[4] Those with this attachment style have a negative view of themselves as well as of others. They are more likely to become substance abusers, abuse their own children, and have mental health problems.

The problem for you, as the child of an alcoholic, is that bonding to your primary caregiver is less likely to have been secure and more likely to have been ambivalent, avoidant, or disorganized.

Without a trustworthy witness to your early life, you have no idea how much the failure to securely attach contributes to your problems today.

Your problems could have originated from something this simple: no one came to hold you when you were afraid, or to pick you up when you cried. Typically, that was your primary caregiver, and typically that person is the enabler.

Children of alcoholics have told us that, in school, they went to sleep each night clutching a pillow to their chest for warmth and comfort, even though the only warmth they received was from their own body.[5]

Harry Harlow would have understood. The lack of warmth from parents is one of those subtle things for which you may be paying the price today.

What Children of Alcoholics Need

One child of an alcoholic told us he used to ask himself what sophisticated knowledge his mother needed to be a good mother. Did she need to fly to New York or Geneva and consult with world famous child psychiatrists?

No, he said, all she needed to do was observe the family dog.

Give the dog attention, pet him, and he thrived. Put him at the end of a chain or ignore him, and he lost heart and chewed on his leg.

This man said he is always amazed by the absolute ordinariness of what it takes to care for a child. Pick the child up, give her attention, now and then help her with her homework, take an interest in her world. "How hard is that?" he asked.

Another child of an alcoholic said, "The concern a mother bear has for her cubs...my mother didn't have that for me."

And if, growing up, you called a friend's mother Mom, it may mean you were looking for the maternal comfort you never received as a child.

Chapter 20

A Deeper Look At Enabling

> Why, sir, for my part I say the gentleman had
> drunk himself out of his five senses.
> —Shakespeare, *The Merry Wives of Windsor*

In the United States, the best-known treatment center for alcoholics is the Hazelden Betty Ford Foundation.

Enabling and Children

The Hazelden Betty Ford Foundation lists these as the five most common codependent and enabling behaviors:[1]
1. Not letting your Loved One face the consequences of addiction
2. Keeping secrets about your Loved One's addiction
3. Not giving your Loved One boundaries and expectations
4. Making excuses for the Loved One's behavior
5. Avoiding the topic of addiction, or avoiding the Loved One

['Loved One' is the foundation's way of talking about an addict.]

Let's crosscheck the foundation's list against the American Psychological Association (APA) definition of enabling. If you recall, the APA says enabling is "a process whereby someone (i.e., the enabler) contributes to continued maladaptive or pathological behavior (e.g., child abuse, substance abuse) in another person."

Based on the APA definition, we think the Hazelden Betty Ford Foundation should add a sixth item to their list.

An enabler is someone who typically does not protect their children from alcoholic maltreatment. (And enablers don't have the excuse of being drunk.)

Usually child maltreatment is a dual failure of the alcoholic and the enabler. The following letter illustrates this...

Hi Wayne & Tamara,

I am a third person looking into a problem that has been plaguing my best friend. She and her husband have been married four years and have two beautiful little boys. One is three years old and the other just three weeks.

Over these years, her husband will go on drinking binges and come home with a very nasty temper. For the most part the abuse has been verbal. He belittles her and tears her down--sometimes disappearing for two or three days at a time and refusing to discuss his actions when he comes home.

I have quietly remained in the background and will offer a sympathetic shoulder for my friend to cry on. I offer her advice the best I can, having been a survivor of an abusive spouse and keeping in mind that the only way things will change is if my friend takes things into her own hands.

However, just recently, I've been put into a situation where not only do I fear for my friend, but her two little boys. I was called over to her house the other night by her parents because her husband had come home completely drunk. He was verbally abusing her and then physically started shoving her. The police were called and by the time I got there, he had taken off with the car, driving drunk.

While talking to the family, I learned there was an instance where they caught the husband driving drunk with the 3-year-old in the car, another where they caught him grabbing the child by the collar, and even further, trying to feed milk too hot for a newborn. All this on top of the normal disregard he shows my friend.

I don't know what to do. I worry for the kids, and I worry for my friend. I don't want to call child services because my friend would lose the very thing she values the most in life.

I want to find just the right words to use to make my friend take a stand in a relationship where she has no voice. She's afraid of being a single mom though she has an incredible support system of family and friends, and most of all, she is trying to save her marriage.

First she thought that having kids would change him, then, maybe a new house, and now a second child. But he hasn't changed and seems to have become more reckless.

Can you offer any words of wisdom I can use when talking to her to give her the strength she needs to do what's right? How can I get her to see what is so obvious to everyone else?

Claire

Claire wrote, "First she thought that having kids would change him, then, maybe a new house, and now a second child. But he hasn't changed and seems to have become more reckless."

Claire's friend is in a casino, using her kids like chips at the craps table. She doesn't value the children; she gambles with them. She puts her drunk husband above the children, and she puts what she wants above anything else.

We don't know how much Claire's kids will suffer at the craps table, but we know they have already lost. They are at the most developmentally sensitive period in their lives. Every day with a drunken father in those formative years can be the death of some part of their potential.

Although Claire's friend doesn't share all the goals of her alcoholic husband, her personal goals coalesce with his. The two adults are cocreators in child maltreatment.

Claire herself is preoccupied with good manners. She is looking for "just the right words" to make her friend wake up. Those words do not exist.

In the U.S., 70% of child maltreatment is reported not by family members, but by professionals who have a legal obligation to do so—police officers, teachers, social workers, and medical personnel.[2] Only 15% of maltreatment is reported by friends, neighbors, or relatives. Unfortunate as that is, between 50 and 90 percent of child maltreatment is never reported.[3]

We hope Claire will take action, even if she has to do it anonymously, because her friend is putting her children at risk.

Risk and Enabling

But what is risk?[4]

Risk is something that creates hazards, and a hazard is anything that can harm us.

Claire's friend is a textbook enabler, and enablers are terrible judges of the level of risk to their children. Her children are at the most critical age of development, and they have already been harmed. The only question is how much more harm will be inflicted on them.

In a classic paper, Ali Siddiq Alhakami and Paul Slovic pointed this out about risk.[5] When people think about an action they want, they view it as having many benefits and low risk. Thinking about an action they do not want, they view it as having low benefit and high risk.

Claire's friend fools herself that staying with her husband is a high benefit, low risk strategy, and she wants to "save her marriage." To do that, she is willing to saddle her children with lifelong problems. That is a defining characteristic of enablers.

Repeatedly, we have heard enablers say, "I don't believe in divorce." What they apparently mean is, "I don't believe in divorce. I believe in putting my children at risk."

We'd like to think the following letter might be written by Claire's friend a few years from now, but we imagine only a different sort of person would write it. The letter is from a woman who realizes that, just as the alcoholic must be brought into alignment with reality, so must the adult living with the alcoholic...

For so long I have been searching for answers. My husband of nine years is an alcoholic/drug addict. His drinking started long before I met him. I became more aware of the severity of his problems during the course of our marriage. It has been a struggle, emotionally and financially.

My husband has three convictions for driving under the influence. He has been through treatment programs twice now.

He recently told me on our ninth anniversary that he wants to be treated normal, like everyone else. He wants the freedom to go and have drinks with the guys and do what he wants, and not be looked down upon.

Of course, when he does make the choice to go out, there are ALWAYS consequences that stem from his night out. He has been beaten, robbed, and left in the middle of nowhere drunk. He has come home bloodied and battered. He has threatened suicide on many occasions, though never attempted it.

Needless to say, I have had many sleepless nights because of him. We have three children together. My oldest, my son, has seen a lot. He has heard the arguing and yelling and seen the tears. I have tried to cover my husband's illness from him. I always tried to clean up the messes for my husband, and am now learning, I have enabled him for years.

I know now I have done him no favors by allowing him to continue this type of behavior. I always believed he would change, with the love of myself and his children. So I stayed.

I gave him that second chance, which now has turned into thousands. I have always been very protective of him. I always thought he is sick, and he doesn't know any better, so he needs someone to help him. I stood by him, time and time again.

Recently, my husband went golfing and apparently drank the entire time. He caused a disturbance in a local bar. He was escorted out by a police officer and ended up running from him. He was handcuffed and brought home to my house where my children witnessed his drunkenness firsthand. It was embarrassing and very disturbing to me.

I will never forget the look on my son's face as long as I live. I feel like I've been a horrible mother, to have put them through all this. I have allowed my husband's illness to destroy our family. It has hurt us emotionally.

My children never asked for this kind of life.

I'm trying to get out now. I want to find peace in my life, and I want my children to be happy and in a home where they can feel safe. I found some of *your articles today, and found a lot of the answers I have been searching for, for so long.*

I just wanted to email you with a warm thanks. I feel as though I can breathe a little easier now, knowing I can't save my husband anymore, knowing he is responsible for saving himself, and knowing I shouldn't feel guilty or ashamed.

You may pass my story on to others if you would like.

Julie

In fairness we must tell you that some people living with an alcoholic are trapped, usually because they come from a dysfunctional background. For example...

I am the mother of a 6-year-old child. My husband is an alcoholic and refuses to realize it because he can skip a few days, once in a while, before drinking again. A few years ago, he went to a counselor with me and was told those few days in between are considered a "dry drunk." I totally agree as his verbal abuse is worst when he's dry occasionally.

I have a little bit of college, but no vehicle or means of getting out on my own. Everyone refuses to help. They tell me to stay with him and raise my son. I feel I am the only parent as my husband spends most of the time drinking, cursing, or sleeping. Why am I the only person who feels this is no life for a child?

My son and I have nowhere to turn. My dad passed away when I was a child. My mother takes as much as she can from us and only looks out for herself. What can I do?

Sondra

We told Sondra...

A few years ago a friend of ours went on vacation, and we agreed to feed his dog, a Great Pyrenees, while he was gone. Wayne was carrying a 50-pound sack of dry dog food through our friend's kitchen, when the bag split. The height and momentum of the moving bag caused dry food to ricochet everywhere.

Dog food covered the entire kitchen floor. Some of it landed in our friend's sun porch, home office, living room, and breakfast nook. It was a mess to clean up, but the hardest part may have been deciding where to start and having the heart to begin.

You are right. This is no life for a child. Your son is growing up in a world totally beyond his control. He can't stop his father's drinking, he can't stop his father's abuse, and his father is not showing him how to be an adult male.

A home like yours is a factory for producing children who will struggle as adults, seeking to please others in preference to seeking workable solutions to problems. In addition, children of alcoholics usually feel isolated and question themselves, while pretending to outsiders that everything is normal.

Your mother won't help. She wants to keep you in this situation for her own benefit. Your friends won't help. The simple aid of close friends and family is unavailable to you, so your first step will have to be a bigger one.

Today, make a list of anyone who can help you. That includes government services, career counselors, women's centers, churches, and an attorney. Look into every possible type of assistance. Tomorrow, you will be contacting everyone on your list. From those contacts your future course will emerge.

Your goal is to get yourself and your son out of the control of an abusive drunk. Keep your eye on the goal. If you go to an organization or individual, and their goal is not the same as yours, move on to the next possibility.

You don't have the ability to make your husband stop drinking, and we are not going to tell you to handcuff yourself to this situation. Some people may tell you that you can help your husband not to drink, but they won't say, as is often the case, you may never change his behavior. He may be five years from sobriety or 35 years from sobriety. He may spend his entire life inside a bottle.

You cannot cure someone of something they deny they have. But you have been cured. You no longer want to be the wife of an alcoholic or have your son raised by one. Don't let anyone uncure you of that.

If you and your son leave, then you control your fate, not a bottle of liquor. Often in life we are handed 50 pounds of dog food to clean up. The hardest part is deciding where to start and having the heart to begin.

Wayne & Tamara

Enablers Fail to Protect Children

You might wonder if we are being too harsh on enablers.

For the moment, let us assume the alcoholic is a man. Wouldn't a comforting woman be able to undo the effects of a father's cruel words? Wouldn't high levels of affection from one parent offset the scorn, ridicule, and humiliation from the other?

No.

That's the clear answer from research.[6] That is what researchers at Harvard, Northeastern University, and McLean Hospital in Belmont, Massachusetts found. In addition, emotional abuse in the form of verbal aggression has lasting effects on brain development.

Using young adults from 18 – 25, with a sample size of 2,518, the research found even if the emotional abuser was later affectionate, it did not offset the harmful effects of the abuse.

While we would love to believe that a 'sainted' enabler can counteract the effects of an alcoholic, we find little evidence that is true.

The point is not that the 'good' parent protects the child; the point is the 'good' parent cannot protect the child. The idea of *good* needs to be refined. How is their goodness not a coverup for their guilt in staying with a person who harms a child? How is it not a coverup for being an agent of harm themselves?

Enablers use three statements of self-delusion to obscure the need for action. "The children don't know." "The children won't understand." "I have to protect the children from this knowledge."

All three remind us of a line from the movie *The Shawshank Redemption*. "Are you being deliberately obtuse?"

Of course, the children know how bad things are.

One woman summed up the responsibility of enablers when she said this about her mother. *I will never understand why she didn't see what staying with my father did to my brother and me. I will never understand why she didn't protect us.*

That is the unexpressed thought of so many children of alcoholics.

Another woman writes...

My final divorce papers sit in front of me waiting for my signature. In fact, they've been sitting on my desk for five days now. It took me two days to even open the envelope and another full day to look at the actual documents. I still haven't entirely read through them. I cannot bring myself to sign.

Eight months ago, after months of emotional turmoil, we both agreed a divorce would be in our best interest. I was relieved at the time. I was tired of him drinking every night until he passed out on the sofa. I was tired of feeling belittled. I never quite healed from the affair I found out about, and I know there were others.

We were married eight years. I never felt I was his partner in life. I felt I was just another piece of furniture. We have two beautiful little boys who adore their daddy. They were a big reason for wanting this divorce. I didn't want them growing up thinking drinking on a daily basis is normal.

For years I wanted counseling. I would plead, "Let's go before our problems get out of control!" He insisted we didn't have anything we couldn't handle. By the time we made it to counseling it was too late. Besides, he refused to say he had an addiction.

I tell myself if he truly reaches out for help and remains changed for a year after our divorce, maybe we could try with a fresh start.

I heard a preacher say, "Fidelity is more than sexual fidelity. It is when every decision you make during the day is the best one for yourself, your spouse, and your children." Wayne and Tamara, that's the only relationship I want.

The papers still sit in front of me. How do I know I'm doing the right thing?
Felicity

Felicity's letter is typical of the letters we receive from enablers.

She is faced with the death of a dream, the dream of what her marriage was supposed to be. She wants to hold onto the dream at the expense of reality.

Her husband is faced with another choice: keep on drinking or lose his family. He continues to drink. She hopes he will change, but she has little reason to believe he will.

Codependency

Previously, we quoted the Hazelden Betty Ford Foundation. When they mention enablers, they also mention codependency, a term which became common with the launch of Melody Beattie's 1987 bestseller *Codependent No More*.

But what is codependency?

In her book, Beattie quotes eight definitions of codependency from eight different people.[7] Then she offers her own definition. To further muddy the waters, Melody Beattie adds, "I'm not trying to confuse you. Codependency has a fuzzy definition because it is a gray, fuzzy condition."

Twenty years later, Beattie published a book called *The New Codependency*. In it she claimed classifying codependency "is still challenging."[8]

Perhaps that is why science writer Maia Szalavitz went so far as to say, "A diagnosis of codependence is about as scientific as a horoscope—and far less interesting."[9]

We would compare the all-purpose way *codependency* is used to baking soda. You can bake with it, and you can use it to deodorize your refrigerator, rinse your mouth, and clean stains off marble.

We don't find the term *codependent* meaningful, though it often appears in discussions of enablers. What the term really refers to is someone who needs to make a change they refuse to consider.

Chapter 21

Adult Children of Alcoholics®

> Your understanding of the problem determines your solution.
> —Bruce Perry, neuroscientist

One group specifically targets adult children of alcoholics for help, but it is a group we do not recommend. Let us explain why.

Adult Children of Alcoholics® (ACA) was founded in 1978.[1]

The primary founder of Adult Children of Alcoholics® was Tony A., an AA member and New York stockbroker. The cofounders were a group of young adults who aged-out of Alateen. For them, Tony created The Laundry List, a list of traits of adult children of alcoholics.

In 1984, Adult Children of Alcoholics® became an autonomous Twelve Step, Twelve Tradition program. The phrase "Twelve Step, Twelve Tradition" has a specific meaning. It refers to two definitive texts of Alcoholics Anonymous.

All three organizations—AA, Al-Anon, and ACA—share the same steps, traditions, and outlook.

Like Alcoholics Anonymous, Adult Children of Alcoholics® has its own bible. It is called the Big Red Book or BRB. The Big Red Book is named for its deep burgundy cover and for its mass. It weighs over 2 lbs. and has 669 numbered pages.

The Problem With Adult Children of Alcoholics®

The foundation of the Adult Children of Alcoholics® (ACA) program is the Twelve Steps, borrowed nearly word for word from Alcoholics Anonymous.²

Briefly, these are the steps they prescribe for children of alcoholics:

1. Admit you're powerless over the effects of alcoholism, and your life is unmanageable.
2. Believe in a Power that can restore you to "sanity."
3. Decide to turn your life and will over to God.
4. Make a searching and fearless moral inventory of yourself.
5. Admit the exact nature of your wrongs to God, yourself, and another person.
6. Stand ready for God to remove your character defects.
7. Humbly ask God to do it.
8. List everyone you've harmed and be prepared to make amends.
9. Make those amends, unless it would make things worse.
10. Continue your personal inventory and admit your mistakes.
11. Pray and meditate so you follow God's will.
12. Carry the Adult Children of Alcoholics® message to others.

The main positive of ACA, for some, is that it provides group support. But we have reservations about ACA for most children of alcoholics.

The first reason is that we always favor data-based, scientific research. Adult Children of Alcoholics®, however, is not a treatment modality. (A treatment modality is a technique or approach used by licensed mental health professionals.) With actual treatment modalities, you can look up success rates.

When we checked research databases, we could not find any reliable statistics on the effectiveness of Adult Children of Alcoholics®. Indeed, while mental health professionals speak of things like affective dysregulation and neuronal loss, ACA speaks of reaching "emotional sobriety," as if the children of alcoholics have been out binging.³

Failures of Adult Children of Alcoholics®

Another obvious problem with Adult Children of Alcoholics® is that the group explicitly faults children of alcoholics.

What other conclusion can you draw from a list telling victims of childhood trauma to take a fearless moral inventory of themselves, admit the exact nature of their wrongs, and ask God to remove their character defects.

At the center of ACA is a false equivalence between the position of the child victim and the position of the adult perpetrators. And, of course, the Twelve Steps were not designed for victims of child maltreatment, any more than programs for rapists are designed for victims of rape.

We can't believe children of alcoholics read the language about moral failings and defects of character and think it applies to them. How many victims of Alcoholic Child Maltreatment don't realize it is another abuse heaped upon them?

That's the basic slander of Adult Children of Alcoholics®. They attempt to graft a program for alcoholics and enablers onto a program for the victims of developmental and relational trauma.

These are the facts in the real world. When, as a result of the home environment, a child...
- dissociates
- is emotionally dysregulated
- suffers complex trauma
- has borderline personality disorder
- has chronically high stress hormones

...the parents get an F in parenting.

ACA does say you can hold family accountable.

This is what they mean by accountability.[4] "We hold our family accountable by naming what happened to us without fear of being ridiculed or disbelieved." The Big Red Book says ACoAs can feel free to talk to their Adult Children of Alcoholics® sponsor or a spiritual advisor about what happened to them.

What ACA means by accountable is simply naming what happened to you. That definition is doublespeak, because it is not what *accountable* means. If it meant that, murderers would merely have to name their crime to be held accountable.

Being accountable means being liable for, and answerable for, one's deeds.

One thing is clear about child maltreatment: we should not wait until the damage is done before intervening in the lives of children. The damage to the children is simply too great, and it will require years of adult life before the damage can be undone, if ever.

Yet Adult Children of Alcoholics® explicitly denies an interest in child welfare programs, legislation, or counseling programs to help victims of childhood abuse and neglect.[5] They say they will not "rally against dysfunctional families." And they add, "In ACA, we learn to keep the focus on ourselves and live and let live."

The Illusory Truth Effect

A friend said this about the right-wing pundit Rush Limbaugh. "You listen to him for a couple of weeks, and he starts to make sense." That statement illustrates a feature of our mind. Repetition of any set of ideas will affect your beliefs.

It's called the illusory truth effect, and it is a form of indoctrination well supported in research.[6] We think it explains why the Big Red Book says, "When possible, we recommend that you attend 60 meetings in 90 days, get a sponsor, and make a start."[7]

Once you are saturated with their viewpoint, you will find it difficult to view your life any other way. To compound the effect, ACA, like Alcoholics Anonymous, offers 'recovery chips' for attendance at meetings and medallions for years of 'emotional sobriety.'

The Motives of Toxic Parents

AA, Al-Anon, and ACA use the slogan "alcoholism is a family disease" for a reason.[8] It obscures the motives of toxic parents. As psychologists Catherine Salmon and Todd Shackelford note, many people don't understand that "Kinship is not one relationship. It is many different relationships."[9]

Remember Claire? Her friend married an alcoholic, then had a child, then a new house, then a second child, hoping her husband would stop drinking. In what way did her motivations illustrate a family system? She was acting for herself, and so was her husband.

The family system idea is primarily useful to genealogists and sociologists. It will be of little use to you.

You have an individual problem, which requires an individual solution. Your nervous system was disrupted by the adults in your life. It will be all you can do to straighten out your own life. Don't get caught up in the additional drama of trying to save your parents, or excuse them, or accept blame for their actions.

Today, ACA has expanded their name. The organization now calls itself Adult Children of Alcoholics® / Dysfunctional Families. That may sound like a plus, because the list of COA traits fits children from virtually any dysfunctional home, as we saw in Chapter 4.

But the overall effect is to drag more victims of child abuse into the network of AA-related Twelve Steps. The sheer unsuitability in trying to apply the steps from Alcoholics Anonymous, to *all* abused and neglected children, takes our breath away.

In the last 40 years, neuroscience has made huge leaps in understanding child abuse and child neglect. That is where the focus should be, not in trying to impose AA's Twelve Steps on children of alcoholics.

The Big Red Book is an example of the fallacy *argumentum verbosium*, which attempts to win an argument through sheer wordiness. As one friend told us, "That book needs an editor!" What she meant is the BRB is a jumble of ideas. The book is full of sweeping generalizations without empirical evidence, and it uses words ambiguously and equivocally.

We began the chapter on Alcoholics Anonymous by quoting John Lilly, who said, "If you want to be an expert, invent the territory." In 1935, Bill Wilson and Bob Smith became 'experts' by inventing the territory of alcoholism.

But extending their Twelve Steps to abused and neglected children is the perfect example of the man with the hammer who sees everything as a nail.

Frankly, we do not trust ACA to protect the interests of children of alcoholics. Whatever merits AA's Twelve Steps may have for alcoholics, it is not a program for children of alcoholics.

In our view, the false note in Adult Children of Alcoholics® / Dysfunctional Families will remain until they divorce themselves from the Twelve Steps of Alcoholics Anonymous.

Your nervous system was profoundly disrupted by your caregivers. You need experts at putting your nervous system back into the normal range. That means people with a deep understanding of neurological and developmental trauma.

That's why we say the place to begin is with psychological and medical practitioners.

Chapter 22

Helpful Apps

> "If you don't know where you are going,
> any road can take you there"
> —Lewis Carroll, *Alice In Wonderland*

There are dozens of mental health apps on the market.[1] Some of them are quite helpful. In this chapter, we preview three of them to give you an idea of their range.

The apps can be used independently, or in conjunction with in-person sessions with a licensed therapist.

Untold – a voice journal. (untoldapp.com)

Untold is a voice journal. You speak what's on your mind into the app, and it displays text soon after you finish speaking. The voice-to-text feature is state of the art, and it is highly accurate, even when you use uncommon words.

If you prefer, you can type your journal, but the voice-to-text feature makes keeping a journal far simpler.

Untold offers writing prompts, and some of the prompts are surprisingly insightful, juxtaposing your own ideas in ways you have never thought of.

Untold is also a friend who wants the best for you. It addresses you by name. As a friend, it will offer you daily meditations and uplifting quotes. It will take elements of your journal and turn them into poetry, flash fiction, or a bedtime story. In addition, it offers you ancient wisdom from a variety of traditions to reflect on.

From your journal entries, the app will help you in cognitive restructuring. That means, using your own statements, it will take what you said and create an argument both for and against a belief you have about yourself. It will then offer a new thought for you to consider.

Untold can also take your journal entries and explain elements of your thoughts from the standpoint of current psychology. If you like looking at your life from the perspective of zodiac signs, enneagrams, or Myer-Briggs, it can do that as well.

Untold is an extremely powerful app that holds up a mirror to your cognitive biases, which are systematic errors in thinking that influence your judgments and decisions.

It is currently free, but a paywall is coming. The developers promise the paywall will be fair.

How We Feel – for emotional self-monitoring (howwefeel.org)

How We Feel is an app which uses emotional self-monitoring to boost your understanding of your feelings and make them easier to regulate.

The basic practice is to record your feelings three times per day, using a screen that maps your current energy level against a wide range of emotions.

There are step-by-step videos to help you reframe your thoughts, regulate your breathing, imagine your best self, build connection to others, and enhance creativity.

Our favorite part of the app is coherent breathing, a breathing exercise with a dynamic visual. It is a powerful centering experience.

The app can also help you use movement to release your emotions, and there are mindfulness and breathing strategies to help you reduce the impact of negative feelings.

The app is free, made possible by donations. Development of the app was led by one of the founders of Pinterest, and the goal of the app is to create a more emotionally healthy world.

InnerWorld – a mental health community (inner.world)

Innerworld is a 24/7, peer support, mental health platform.

In this virtual community, members use avatars to navigate between different worlds. The app enables participants to attend dozens of weekly sessions led by trained guides and/or small weekly sessions led by therapists.

The guide-led events run daily and cover a wide range of topics. There are support groups which focus on conflict resolution, depression, social anxiety, grief, dream analysis, ADHD, meditation, addiction recovery, and more. The guide-led events usually last about an hour.

There are three different activity tiers in InnerWorld.

—Free: For those looking to explore Innerworld, the free tier offers access to a common area and all social events.

—Membership: A low-cost tier offering access to all guide-led mental health events.

—Membership Plus: A little more expensive tier including everything in the membership tier, plus a weekly 80 minute group session with a licensed therapist. The therapist-led groups are called Innercircles.

There is another tool worth mentioning: mindfulness. Mindfulness is the practice of paying attention to the present moment, without judgment. This is usually done by simply following your breath as you breathe in and out. Over time, this practice will allow you to see the world and your life with fresh eyes. As one therapist said to us, "Mindfulness is about finding the silence in your mind."

Mindfulness is incorporated into many mental health apps, and we have suggested books on mindfulness on the Resources page. The books vary in their approach.

Chapter 23

Conclusion

> "It's too late to make things different for me, but if somebody understands how awful it really is, maybe they will help some other kids."[1]
> —Peter, age 15, child of an alcoholic

We began this book by listening to three children of alcoholics.

Leah wondered if it would be okay if she drank a glass of wine at the end of each day. She was astounded to think that her question could have anything to do with her mother's alcoholism.

We would not say Leah requires therapy. But if she wants to understand the milestones in her life, Leah could learn a lot through guided journaling, discussing her key decisions with trusted friends, and through counseling.

Frank, on the other hand, was a high achiever in school who lost his job as a lawyer and now doesn't feel worthy of being hired. He needs a psychotherapist and perhaps now a career coach.

Finally, Tara was a woman in complete emotional collapse. She said, "I don't understand what's going on with me. In general, I guess, I have lost my personality because I cannot feel who am I, what I like, what am I going to do, what I want, who I want to be, and what is my point of life?"

Tara's upbringing was a scourge. She desperately needs psychological help, and that may mean taking a break from her studies.

We have always enjoyed *The Wonderful Tar Baby*, Joel Chandler Harris' story about a rabbit and the fox who tried to catch him.

To trap Brer Rabbit, Brer Fox made a realistic baby from tar and turpentine, and set it on a stump. Then he hid in the bushes. When Brer Rabbit came along, he tried to be sociable. He said "Morning" to the tar baby, but the tar baby said nothing.

Again and again, Brer Rabbit tried to be friendly, and each time the tar baby said nothing.

At last, Brer Rabbit grew angry at this rudeness. He hauled off and hit the tar baby, and got his fist stuck in tar. Then the rabbit hit him again and got his other fist stuck. The more Brer Rabbit tussled with the tar baby, the more stuck he got.

If you are the child of an alcoholic, your family is your tar baby. Often, the more you engage with them, the deeper you will get stuck.

In the end, Brer Rabbit got the last laugh by outwitting the fox.

Your way of getting the last laugh is to stop being a victim. That means more than simply healing. It means never allowing anyone to treat you that way again.

At the end of Ernest Hemingway's novel *The Sun Also Rises*, one character summarizes the story by saying, "We could have had such a damn good time together." That's the way children of alcoholics often feel about their family. We could have had such a damn good time together.

But we didn't, because my parents broke the compact of care between parent and child.

That is not, however, a reason why you shouldn't have a good life.

A Brief Note

If you found this book helpful, please leave an honest review where you purchased it. That will help other children of alcoholics find *As the Child of an Alcoholic*.

Thank you,

Wayne & Tamara

About the authors

For over 20 years, Wayne and Tamara Mitchell wrote the advice column *Direct Answers*. Their column appeared in newspapers in more than a dozen countries.

As one reader wrote, "I found your column several years ago by accident but read it regularly. You provide the most clear, concise, gender neutral and useful answers."

Wayne and Tamara Mitchell are also the authors of *Cheating in a Nutshell* and *The Young Woman's Guide to Older Men*.

Resources

Anxiety and Fear
Rewire Your Anxious Brain, by Catherine Pittman and Elizabeth Karle
50 Ways to Rewire Your Anxious Brain, by Catherine Pittman and Maha Zayed Hoffman
Afraid: Understanding the Purpose of Fear and Harnessing the Power of Anxiety, by Arash Javanbakht
There Is Nothing Wrong with You, by Cheri Huber

Depression
Retrain Your Brain: Cognitive Behavioral Therapy in 7 Weeks: a Workbook for Managing Depression and Anxiety, by Seth Gillihan
Don't Believe Everything You Think: Why Your Thinking Is The Beginning & End of Suffering, by Joseph Nguyen

Trauma
Complex PTSD, by Pete Walker.
The Complex PTSD Workbook, by Arielle Schwartz
The Grief That Dare Not Speak Its Name, Parts I, II, and III, three essays by Sandra Bloom (currently available online)
The Body Keeps the Score, by Bessel van der Kolk

Parents
Toxic Parents, by Susan Forward
Adult Children of Emotionally Immature Parents, by Lindsay Gibson
But It's Your Family, by Sherrie Campbell
Emotional Blackmail, by Susan Forward
Healing Your Lost Inner Child, by Robert Jackman

The Emotionally Absent Mother, by Jasmin Lee Cori.

The Nervous System
What Happened to You? Conversations on Trauma, Resilience, and Healing, by Bruce Perry and Oprah Winfrey
Anchored: How to Befriend Your Nervous System Using Polyvagal Theory, by Deb Dana

Boundaries
The Set Boundaries Workbook, by Nedra Glover Tawwab

Borderline Personality Disorder
Understanding the Borderline Mother, by Christine Lawson

Dissociation
Coping with Trauma-Related Dissociation, by Suzette Boon, Kathy Steele, and Onno van der Hart

Recovery from Sexual Abuse
The Courage to Heal, by Ellen Bass and Laura Davis

Coaching
Positive Intelligence, by Shirzad Chamine
The One Thing, by Gary Keller

Mindfulness
Mindfulness in Plain English, by Bhante Gunaratana
A Walk in the Wood, by Joseph and Nancy Parent
Practicing Mindfulness, by Matthew Sockolov
Zen Mind, Beginners Mind, by Shunryu Suzuki

Chapter Notes

Chapter 1 - Introduction
1. National Institute on Alcohol Abuse and Alcoholism (Apr 2021).

Chapter 2 – Three Children
1. Werner (1993). "Children who succeeded against the odds had the opportunity to establish, early on, a close bond with at least one competent, emotionally stable person who was sensitive to their needs."
Walker (2013) p 93. "Traumatic emotional neglect occurs when a child does not have a single caretaker to whom she can turn in times of need or danger."
When Jessica Goeke interviewed eight adult children of alcoholics, she found another protective factor. A close sibling relationship. When the kids stick together, they can help each other survive. Goeke (2017)

Chapter 3 - An Outdated Book
1. Woititz, Janet (1983) p 4.
2. Woititz, Lisa Sue (2015) p 1.
3. Ibid. p 4.
4. The American Psychological Association definition of Enabling (2024).

Chapter 4 – Two Underlying Ideas
1. Arielle Schwartz, The Complex PTSD Workbook, Chapter 1.
2. Herndon (2024); Raising Children Network (2024).
3. Murray, Desiree (2015); Rosenbalm, K. D (2017); Beeghly, Perry, and Tronick (2016); Tronick and Perry (2015).
4. Center on the Developing Child (2024); Karbach and Unger (2014).

5. Schwartz (2021)
6. Seefeldt (1992); Fisher et al. (1993); Harter (2000); Manley (2015).
7. Clinton (2004), Chapter 3.

Chapter 5 – That-Which-Must-Not-Be-Named
1. Preface to the first edition of the Big Book.
2. Leeb et al. (2011)
3. Child Welfare Information Gateway (2018); U.S. Department of Health & Human Services, Child Maltreatment (2019).
4. Child Welfare Information Gateway (2018)
5. Grant (2000); American Academy of Child and Adolescent Psychiatry (2019).

Consider this. "Approximately 53 percent of Americans have one or more close relatives who have an alcohol dependency problem. In addition, 43 percent of American adults have been exposed to the problem of alcoholism in the family, either as something they grew up with or something they experienced with a spouse or a partner." *Alcoholism Statistics and Important Facts* by Lizmarie Maldonado, a biostatistician. American Addiction Centers, November 1, 2023. Accessed 17 Feb 2024.

6. Lander et al. (2013)
7. Putnam (2006)
8. Shonkoff et al. (2011); Putnam (2006); National Scientific Council Working Paper (2020); National Scientific Council Working Paper (2008); Teicher et al. (2016); Teicher et al. (2021); Kelly-Irving (2019); Ellis and Del Giudice (2013); Beauchaine et al. (2011); Chen and Baram (2015); Thayer et al. (2016); Danese and McEwen (2012).
9. Centers for Disease Control and Prevention (2019)
10. The above report from the Centers for Disease Control and Prevention (CDC) indicated toxic stress in childhood "can even alter the physical structure of DNA." Frank Putnam, previously cited, referenced a paper that reported exposure to domestic violence can have twice the effect on a child's IQ as exposure to environmental lead.
11. Felitti et al. (1998)
12. Teicher et al. (2016)
13. Nolan et al. (2020)

14. National Scientific Council Working Paper (2008)
15. Manley (2015); Harter (2000); Seefeldt and Lyon (1992).
16. Perry (2017)

Chapter 6 - Trauma
1. The dates for the war vary. We chose to use the Gulf of Tonkin Resolution as the beginning event, and the full withdrawal of American troops as the final event.
2. Crocq and Crocq (2000); Bloom (2000a).

Chapter 7 – Complex Trauma
1. Herman (1992)
2. Walker (2017) Glossary.
3. National Health Service (2021) "Complex PTSD - Post-traumatic stress disorder."
4. Repetti et al. (2002). As the UCLA researchers wrote, "By adolescence, the offspring of risky families must adapt to the cumulative consequences of years spent in a damaging home environment."

Chapter 8 – What Needs Healing
Verlyn Klinkenborg, *Several Short Sentences About Writing*, p 2.
1. Ireton et al. (2024)
2. NeuroscienceNews.com (2024)
3. Anda et al. (2002)
4. Venegas (2021)
5. National Education Alliance for Borderline Personality Disorder (2024); Gvirts et al. (2012); Ghanem et al. (2016).
6. Porter et al. (2019); Ford and Courtois (2021).
7. Boon et al. (2011), p 9.
8. Kappes and Oettingen (2011)

Chapter 9 – 'Great Parents'
Euripides: Found in Ovid's Toyshop of the Heart: Epistulae Heroidum by Florence Verducci, Princeton (1985).

1. Goodrich, Robert (1998, 1999a, 1999b); Associated Press (1997a, 1997b).
2. Shengold (1991), p 26.

Chapter 10 – Facing Facts
Quiller Couch: Armistice Day Anniversary Sermon (1923)
1. Pete Walker (2013), Chapters 2, 11.
2. Bloom (2000c)
3. Bloom (2000b, c, d)

Chapter 11 – The Nervous System, Part 1
1. Kelly-Irving (2019)
2. Palo Alto Weekly Staff (2018)
3. Perry and Szalavitz (2017), Introduction.
4. Douglas (2021); Tronick and Perry (2015).
5. Douglas (2021)
6. Perry and Winfrey (2021), p 26.
7. Perry (2001)
8. Beeghly et al. (2016); Tronick and Perry (2015).
9. Perry (2001)

Chapter 12 – The Nervous System, Part 2
1. Dana (2021)
2. Dana (2018) Section 1 Befriending the Nervous System; Lyon (2016); Porges (1995); Porges (2021).

Chapter 13 – Shame
Richardson: *Take Heart, Illiterates*
1. Kammerer (2019); Straussner (2011); Lander (2013).

Chapter 14 – Recalibration, An Overview
The Expanse, Season 6, episode 5, Time 12:30.
1. Drew (2020)
2. Barnes and Wilson (2010)
3. Sullivan (2024)

Chapter 16 – Boundaries
1. Winfrey (1993), Time 29:56.

Chapter 17 – Understanding Yourself
1. Arlinghaus and Johnston (2018)
2. Ingermanson (2022)

Chapter 18 – Alcoholics Anonymous
Lilly quote: Smith, Adam. *Powers of Mind*. New York: Random House. 1975, p 297.
1. A good history of AA can be found in Bufe (1991), Chapters 2 and 3.
2. Wing (1981)
3. Ibid.
4. Jellinek (1960)
5. Babor (1996)
6. Ibid.
7. Bufe (1991), pp 35-38.
8. John 14:6
9. Mark 16:15
10. Sinclair (2019), p xxi.
11. Pressfield and Coyne (2012), p 34.
12. Maté (2011), p 136.
13. Satel and Lilienfeld (2014)
14. Fingarette (1989), p 112.
15. Grant et al. (2017)
16. Chapman et al. (2015)
17. National Institute on Alcohol Abuse and Alcoholism (2007)
18. Heather (2020)
19. Grant (2000)

Chapter 19 – Enablers And Bonding
1. Harlow and Zimmerman (1958); Harlow (1958); Harlow, Dodsworth, and Harlow (1965); Vicedo (2009) (2010).

2. Karen (1994). Summary pp 5-9, 444-45; Overview of the research: 87-102, 119-125, 143-161.
3. Cherry (2023).
4. Reisz et al. (2017)
5. Repetti et al. (2002)

Chapter 20 – A Deeper Look At Enabling
1. Hazelden Betty Ford Foundation (2021).
2. U.S. Department of Health & Human Services (2024)
3. Leeb et al. (2011)
4. Repetti et al. (2002)
5. Alhakami and Slovic (1994)
6. Polcari et al. (2014); Kim et al. (2019).
7. Beattie (1986), Chapter 3.
8. Beattie (2010), Chapter 3.
9. Szalavitz (2016), p 151.

Chapter 21 – Adult Children of Alcoholics®
Perry (2017), p 700.
1. Today they are incorporated under the name Adult Children of Alcoholics® & Dysfunctional Families World Service Organization, Inc.
2. Tony A. published his own version of the Twelve Steps in 1991. ACA Fellowship Text (aka The Big Red Book) (2006) p xxxvi. Some ACA groups use his version.
3. ACA Fellowship Text (2006), p 265.
4. Ibid. p 157.
5. Ibid. pp xvi-xvii.
6. Hassan and Barber (2021); The Decision Lab (2022).
7. ACA Fellowship Text (2006), p 125.
8. That is right from Tony A's Laundry List. He claimed, "alcoholism is a family disease." ACA Fellowship Text (2006), p 6. That is something AA, Al-Anon, and ACA all do.
9. Salmon and Shackelford (2007)

Chapter 22 – Helpful Apps

1. King et al. (2023). The number of apps might be in the thousands.

Chapter 23 – Conclusion
1. Cork (1969), p 19. Unfortunately, her book is as timely today as when it was published.

References

A., Tony, and Dan F. 1990. *The Laundry List*. Deerfield Beach, FL: Health Communications.

Alhakami, Ali Siddiq, and Paul Slovic. 1994. "A Psychological Study of the Inverse Relationship between Perceived Risk and Perceived Benefit." *Risk Analysis* 14 (6): 1085–96.

American Academy of Child and Adolescent Psychiatry. 2019. "Alcohol Use in Families, No. 17." Washington DC: The American Academy of Child and Adolescent Psychiatry.

American Psychological Association Dictionary of Psychology. 2024. "Enabling." Accessed 24 Nov 2024. dictionary.apa.org.

Anda, Robert F., Charles L. Whitfield, Vincent J. Felitti, Daniel Chapman, Valerie J. Edwards, Shanta R. Dube, and David F. Williamson. 2002. "Adverse Childhood Experiences, Alcoholic Parents, and Later Risk of Alcoholism and Depression." *Psychiatric Services* 53 (8): 1001–9.

Anderson, Frank G. 2021. *Transcending Trauma: Healing Complex PTSD with Internal Family Systems*. Eau Claire, WI: Pesi Publishing.

Anon. 2004. "My Brave Heart." Submission to: Australian Federal Government Senate Inquiry Into Children in Institutional Care 1920-1970.

Anon. 2006. *ACA Fellowship Text (The Big Red Book)*. Signal Hill CA: ACAWSO.

Arlinghaus, Katherine R., and Craig A. Johnston. 2018. "The Importance of Creating Habits and Routine." *American Journal of Lifestyle Medicine* 13 (2): 142–44.

Associated Press. 1997a. "Stepmother Indicted in 1961 Death." *Telegraph Herald* (Dubuque IA), February 8, 1997.

———. 1997b. "Woman Indicted in Stepdaughter's 1961 Stomping Death." *Fort Worth Star-Telegram*, February 9, 1997.

Babor, Thomas. 1996. "The Classification of Alcoholics: Typology Theories from the 19th Century to the Present." *Alcohol Health & Research World* 20 (1).

Bale, Tracy L. 2015. "Epigenetic and Transgenerational Reprogramming of Brain Development." *Nature Reviews Neuroscience* 16 (6): 332–44.

Barnes, Mary Ellen, and Edward Wilson. 2010. "Why AA and Alanon Are Bad for Your Health." May 12, 2010. Accessed 2 Jan 2024. non12step.com.

Bavelier, Daphne, Dennis Levi, Roger Li, Yang Dan, and Takao Hensch. 2010. "Removing Brakes on Adult Brain Plasticity: From Molecular to Behavioral Interventions." *Journal of Neuroscience* 30 (45): 14964–71.

Beattie, Melody. 1986. *Codependent No More: How to Stop Controlling Others and Start Caring for Yourself.* Center City, MN: Hazelden Publishing.

———. 2010. *The New Codependency: Help and Guidance for Today's Generation.* New York: Simon & Schuster.

Beauchaine, Theodore P., Emily Neuhaus, Maureen Zalewski, Sheila E. Crowell, and Natalia Potapova. 2011. "The Effects of Allostatic Load on Neural Systems Subserving Motivation, Mood Regulation, and Social Affiliation." *Development and Psychopathology* 23 (4): 975–99.

Beeghly, Marjorie, Bruce Perry, and Edward Tronick. 2016. "Self-Regulatory Processes in Early Development." In *The Oxford Handbook of Treatment Processes and Outcomes in Psychology*, edited by Sara Maltzman. Oxford Handbooks Online.

Black, Claudia. 1981. *It Will Never Happen to Me.* Denver, CO: M.A.C. Printing And Publications Division.

Bloom, Sandra. 1997. *Creating Sanctuary: Toward the Evolution of Sane Societies.* New York: Routledge.

———. 2000a. "Chapter 3 - Our Hearts and Our Hopes Are Turned to Peace." In *International Handbook of Human Response to Trauma*, edited by A. Shalev, R. Yehuda, and A. McFarlane. New York: Kluwer/Plenum.

———. 2000b. "Dealing with the Ravages of Childhood Abuse Part I." *The Psychotherapy Review* 2 (9).

———. 2000c. "Dealing with the Ravages of Childhood Abuse Part II." *The Psychotherapy Review* 2 (10).

———. 2000d. "Dealing with the Ravages of Childhood Abuse Part III." *The Psychotherapy Review* 2 (11).

Bonanno, George A. 2021. *The End of Trauma: How the New Science of Resilience Is Changing How We Think about PTSD*. New York: Basic Books.

Boon, Suzette, Kathy Steele, and Onno van der Hart. 2011. *Coping with Trauma-Related Dissociation: Skills Training for Patients and Their Therapists*. New York: W.W. Norton.

Bradshaw, John. 1988. *Healing the Shame That Binds You*. Deerfield Beach, FL: Health Communications.

Brazelton, T. Berry, and Stanley I. Greenspan. 2000. *The Irreducible Needs of Children: What Every Child Must Have to Grow, Learn, and Flourish*. Cambridge, MA: Perseus.

Brian, Tracy. 2010. *Goals!* 2nd ed. San Francisco: Berrett-Koehler.

Bufe, Charles. 1991. *Alcoholics Anonymous: Cult or Cure?* San Francisco: See Sharp Press.

Center on the Developing Child (Harvard University). 2024. "What Is Executive Function? And How Does It Relate to Child Development." Accessed 3 Jun 2024. developingchild.harvard.edu

Centers for Disease Control and Prevention. 2019. "Preventing Adverse Childhood Experiences: Leveraging the Best Available Evidence." Atlanta, GA: National Center for Injury Prevention and Control, Centers for Disease Control and Prevention.

Chapman, Cath, Tim Slade, Caroline Hunt, and Maree Teesson. 2015. "Delay to First Treatment Contact for Alcohol Use Disorder." *Drug and Alcohol Dependence* 147 (February): 116–21.

Chen, Yuncai, and Tallie Z. Baram. 2015. "Toward Understanding How Early-Life Stress Reprograms Cognitive and Emotional Brain Networks." *Neuropsychopharmacology* 41 (1): 197–206.

Cherry, Kendra. 2023. "The Different Types of Attachment Styles." Very Well Mind. December 14, 2023. Accessed 18 Jan 2024. verywellmind.com.

Child Welfare Information Gateway. 2018. "Acts of Omission: An Overview of Child Neglect." Washington DC: U.S. Department of Health and Human Services, Children's Bureau.

Clear, James. 2018. *Atomic Habits.* New York: Penguin Random House.

Clinton, Bill. 2004. *My Life.* New York: Random House.

Cohen, Emily, Richard Feinn, Albert Arias, and Henry R. Kranzler. 2007. "Alcohol Treatment Utilization: Findings from the National Epidemiologic Survey on Alcohol and Related Conditions." *Drug and Alcohol Dependence* 86 (2-3): 214–21.

Cohen, Patricia, and Jacob Cohen. 1984. "The Clinician's Illusion." *Archives of General Psychiatry* 41 (12): 1178.

Cole, Trena. 2002. *Charred Souls: A Story of Recreational Child Abuse.* Indianapolis, IN: Oberpark.

Cork, Margaret. 1969. *The Forgotten Children.* Toronto, ON: Alcoholism & Drug Addiction Research Foundation.

Crocq, Marc-Antoine, and Louis Crocq. 2000. "From Shell Shock and War Neurosis to Posttraumatic Stress Disorder: A History of Psychotraumatology." *Dialogues in Clinical Neuroscience* 2 (1).

Dana, Deb. 2018. *The Polyvagal Theory in Therapy: Engaging the Rhythm of Regulation.* New York: W.W. Norton.

———. 2021. *Anchored: How to Befriend Your Nervous System Using Polyvagal Theory.* Boulder, CO: Sounds True.

Danese, Andrea, and Bruce S. McEwen. 2012. "Adverse Childhood Experiences, Allostasis, Allostatic Load, and Age-Related Disease." *Physiology & Behavior* 106 (1): 29–39.

Double, Kate. 2021. "The Co-Regulation Effect." Relationship Restoration. April 12, 2021. Accessed 23 Nov 2024. relationshiprestoration.org.

Douglas, Allison Cooke. 2021. "Meeting Children Where They Are: The Neurosequential Model of Therapeutics." Adoption Advocate, Issue 160. National Council for Adoption, Alexandria VA. October 2021.

Drew, Liam. 2020. "Random Search Wired into Animals May Help Them Hunt." *Quanta Magazine,* June 11, 2020.

Eisenberger, Naomi I. 2012. "The Pain of Social Disconnection: Examining the Shared Neural Underpinnings of Physical and Social Pain." *Nature Reviews Neuroscience* 13 (6): 421–34.

Eisenberger, Naomi, and Matthew Lieberman. 2005. "Why It Hurts to Be Left Out: The Neurocognitive Overlap between Physical and Social Pain." *Sydney Symposium of Social Psychology*, 2005.

Ellis, Bruce J., and Marco Del Giudice. 2013. "Beyond Allostatic Load: Rethinking the Role of Stress in Regulating Human Development." *Development and Psychopathology* 26 (1): 1–20.

Fan, Amy Z., Sanchen Patricia Chou, Haitao Zhang, Jeesun Jung, and Bridget F. Grant. 2019. "Prevalence and Correlates of Past-Year Recovery from DSM-5 Alcohol Use Disorder: Results from National Epidemiologic Survey on Alcohol and Related Conditions-III." *Alcoholism: Clinical and Experimental Research* 43 (11): 2406–20.

Felitti, Vincent J., Robert F. Anda, Dale Nordenberg, David F. Williamson, Alison M. Spitz, Valerie Edwards, Mary P. Koss, and James S. Marks. 1998. "Relationship of Childhood Abuse and Household Dysfunction to Many of the Leading Causes of Death in Adults." *American Journal of Preventive Medicine* 14 (4): 245–58.

Fineran, Kerrie, John M. Laux, Jennifer Seymour, and Tequilla Thomas. 2009. "The Barnum Effect and Chaos Theory: Exploring College Student ACOA Traits." *Journal of College Student Psychotherapy* 24 (1):17–31.

Fingarette, Herbert. 1989. *Heavy Drinking: the Myth of Alcoholism as a Disease*. Berkeley, CA: University Of California Press.

Fisher, Gary L., Stephen J. Jenkins, Thomas C. Harrison, and Kelly Jesch. 1993. "Personality Characteristics of Adult Children of Alcoholics, Other Adults from Dysfunctional Families, and Adults from Nondysfunctional Families." *International Journal of the Addictions* 28(5): 477–85.

Foo, Stephanie. 2022. *What My Bones Know: A Memoir of Healing from Complex Trauma*. New York: Random House.

Ford, Julian D., and Christine A. Courtois. 2021."Complex PTSD and Borderline Personality Disorder." *Borderline Personality Disorder and Emotion Dysregulation* 8 (1).

Ghanem, Mohamed, Doha El-Serafi, Walaa Sabry, Amany Haroun El-Rasheed, Ghada Abdel Razek, Alaa Soliman, and Wafaa Amar. 2016."Executive Dysfunctions in Borderline Personality Disorder." *Middle East Current Psychiatry* 23 (2): 85–92.

Gibson, Lindsay C. 2020. *Who You Were Meant to Be: A Guide to Finding or Recovering Your Life's Purpose*. Second Edition. Virginia Beach, VA: Blue Bird Press.

Glaser, Gabrielle. 2015. "The Irrationality of Alcoholics Anonymous." *The Atlantic*, April 2015.

Goeke, Jessica. 2017. "Identifying Protective Factors for Adult Children of Alcoholics." Thesis, Sophia, the St. Catherine University repository website.

Goldstein, Sam, Jack Naglieri, Dana Princiotta, and Tulio Otero. 2014. "Introduction: A History of Executive Functioning as a Theoretical and Clinical Construct." In *Handbook of Executive Functioning*, edited by Sam Goldstein and Jack Naglieri, 3–12. New York: Springer.

Goodrich, Robert. 1998. "Stepmother Pleads Guilty in Girl's 1961 Death - Murder Charge Is Reduced to Involuntary Manslaughter." *St. Louis Post-Dispatch*, October 21, 1998.

———. 1999a. "Stepmother Gets 5 Years for Stomping Girl to Death - She Had Pleaded Guilty to '61 Killing of 4-Year-Old in Home near Mascoutah." *St. Louis Post-Dispatch*, May 11, 1999.

———. 1999b. "Guilty Plea That Ended 1961 Case of Deadly Child Abuse Answers Few Questions." *St. Louis Post-Dispatch*, May 12, 1999.

Grant, Bridget. 2000. "Estimates of US Children Exposed to Alcohol Abuse and Dependence in the Family." *American Journal of Public Health* 90 (1): 112–15.

Grant, Bridget F., S. Patricia Chou, Tulshi D. Saha, Roger P. Pickering, Bradley T. Kerridge, W. June Ruan, Boji Huang, et al. 2017."Prevalence of 12-Month Alcohol Use, High-Risk Drinking, and DSM-IV Alcohol Use Disorder in the United States, 2001-2002 to 2012-2013."*JAMA Psychiatry* 74 (9): 911.

Gray, Kurt, and Daniel M. Wegner. 2008. "The Sting of Intentional Pain." *Psychological Science* 19 (12): 1260–62.

Greene, Melissa Fay. 2020. "30 Years Ago, Romania Deprived Thousands of Babies of Human Contact." *The Atlantic*, July 2020.

Guidi, Jenny, Marcella Lucente, Nicoletta Sonino, and Giovanni A. Fava. 2020. "Allostatic Load and Its Impact on Health: A Systematic Review." *Psychotherapy and Psychosomatics* 90 (August): 1–17.

Gvirts, Hila, Hagai Harari, Yoram Braw, Daphna Shefet, Simone Shamay-Tsoory, and Yechiel Levkovitz. 2012. "Executive Functioning among Patients with Borderline Personality Disorder (BPD) and Their Relatives." *Journal of Affective Disorders* 143 (1-3): 261–64.

Harlow, H. F., and R. R. Zimmerman. 1958. "The Development of Affective Responsiveness in Infant Monkeys." *Proceedings of the American Philosophical Society*, 102, 501–9.

Harlow, Harry. 1958. "The Nature of Love." *American Psychologist* 13 (673–685).

Harlow, Harry, Robert Dodsworth, and Margaret Harlow. 1965. "Total Social Isolation in Monkeys." *Proceedings of the National Academy of Sciences* 54 (1): 90–97.

Harmer, Bonnie, Sarah Lee, TVH. Duong, and Abdolreza Saadabadi. 2021. "Suicidal Ideation." Treasure Island, FL: StatPearls Publishing.

Harter, Stephanie Lewis. 2000. "Psychosocial Adjustment of Adult Children of Alcoholics." *Clinical Psychology Review* 20 (3): 311–37.

Hassan, Aumyo, and Sarah J. Barber. 2021. "The Effects of Repetition Frequency on the Illusory Truth Effect." *Cognitive Research: Principles and Implications* 6 (1).

Hazelden Betty Ford Foundation. 2021. "What Is Enabling?" September 7, 2021. Accessed 11 Nov 2024. hazeldenbettyford.org.

Heather, Nick. 1992. "Why Alcoholism Is Not a Disease." *Medical Journal of Australia* 156 (3): 212–15.

———. 2020. "Let's Not Turn Back the Clock: Comments on Kelly et al., 'Alcoholics Anonymous and 12-Step Facilitation Treatments for Alcohol Use Disorder: A Distillation of a 2020 Cochrane Review for Clinicians and Policy Makers.'" *Alcohol and Alcoholism* 56 (4): 377–79.

Herman, Judith Lewis. 1992. "Complex PTSD: A Syndrome in Survivors of Prolonged and Repeated Trauma." *Journal of Traumatic Stress* 5 (3): 377–91.

Herndon, Jaime. 2024. "What Is Self-Regulation?" *VeryWell Health*, January 20, 2024. Accessed 24 Nov 2024. verywellhealth.com.

Center on the Developing Child at Harvard University. "In Brief: Connecting the Brain to the Rest of the Body." n.d. Accessed 13 Oct 2024. developingchild.harvard.edu.

Ingermanson, Randy. 2022. "What to Do When You're Overwhelmed." Advanced Fiction Writing. July 19, 2022. Accessed 23 Nov 2024 advancedfictionwriting.com.

Ireton, Rebecca, Anna Hughes, and Megan Klabunde. 2024. "An FMRI Meta-Analysis of Childhood Trauma." *Biological Psychiatry: Cognitive Neuroscience and Neuroimaging* 9 (6): 561–70.

Jellinek, E M. 1960. *The Disease Concept of Alcoholism*. New Haven, CT: Hillhouse.

Julian, Kate. 2021. "America Has a Drinking Problem." *The Atlantic*, July 2021.

Kammerer, Annette. 2019. "The Scientific Underpinnings and Impacts of Shame." *Scientific American*, August 9, 2019.

Kappes, Heather Barry, and Gabriele Oettingen. 2011. "Positive Fantasies about Idealized Futures Sap Energy." *Journal of Experimental Social Psychology* 47 (4): 719–29.

Karbach, Julia, and Kerstin Unger. 2014. "Executive Control Training from Middle Childhood to Adolescence." *Frontiers in Psychology* 5 (May).

Karen, Robert. 1994. *Becoming Attached: First Relationships and How They Shape Our Capacity to Love*. New York: Oxford University Press.

Kelly-Irving, Michelle. 2019. "Allostatic Load: How Stress in Childhood Affects Life-Course Health Outcomes, Working Paper #3." London: The Health Foundation.

Kim, Dohyun, Jae Hyun Yoo, Young Woo Park, Minchul Kim, Dong Woo Shin, and Bumseok Jeong. 2019. "Anatomical and Neurochemical Correlates of Parental Verbal Abuse: A Combined MRS—Diffusion MRI Study." *Frontiers in Human Neuroscience* 13 (January).

Kim-Spoon, Jungmeen, Toria Herd, Alexis Brieant, Kristin Peviani, Kirby Deater-Deckard, Nina Lauharatanahirun, Jacob Lee, and Brooks King-Casas. 2021. "Maltreatment and Brain Development: The Effects of Abuse and Neglect on Longitudinal Trajectories of Neural Activation during Risk Processing and Cognitive Control." *Developmental Cognitive Neuroscience* 48 (April): 100939.

King, Darlene R., Margaret R. Emerson, Julia Tartaglia, Geeta Nanda, and Nathan Tatro. 2023. "Methods for Navigating the Mobile Mental Health App Landscape for Clinical Use." *Current Treatment Options in Psychiatry* 10 (2): 72–86.

Koenen, Karestan, Terrie Moffitt, Avshalom Caspi, Alan Taylor, and Shaun Purcell. 2003. "Domestic Violence Is Associated with Environmental Suppression of IQ in Young Children." *Development and Psychopathology* 15 (2): 297–311.

Koenig, Laura B., Jon Randolph Haber, and Theodore Jacob. 2020. "Transitions in Alcohol Use over Time: A Survival Analysis." *BMC Psychology* 8 (1).

Kross, E., M. G. Berman, W. Mischel, E. E. Smith, and T.D. Wager. 2011. "Social Rejection Shares Somatosensory Representations with Physical Pain." *Proceedings of the National Academy of Sciences* 108 (15): 6270–75.

Lander, Laura, Janie Howsare, and Marilyn Byrne. 2013. "The Impact of Substance Use Disorders on Families and Children: From Theory to Practice." *Social Work in Public Health* 28 (3-4): 194–205.

Leeb, Rebecca, Terri Lewis, and Adam Zolotor. 2011. "A Review of Physical and Mental Health Consequences of Child Abuse and Neglect and Implications for Practice." *American Journal of Lifestyle Medicine*, August.

Lewis, Marc D. 2015. *The Biology of Desire: Why Addiction Is Not a Disease*. New York: Public Affairs.

Lissy, Kara. 2021. *Adult Children of Alcoholic Parents: An Evidence-Based Workbook to Heal Your Past*. Emeryville, CA: Rockridge Press.

Lyon, Bret. 2016. "Anatomy of a Freeze – or Dorsal Vagal Shutdown." Center for Healing Shame. January 16, 2016. Accessed 23 Nov 2024. healingshame.com.

Manley, Valerie. 2015. "Clinical Perspectives on the Applicability of 'ACOA' as a Diagnosis." Thesis, Georgia State University.

Maté, Gabor. 2011. *In the Realm of Hungry Ghosts: Close Encounters with Addiction*. Berkeley, CA: North Atlantic Books.

McEwen, Bruce. 2000. "Allostasis and Allostatic Load Implications for Neuropsychopharmacology." *Neuropsychopharmacology* 22 (2): 108–24.

———. 2006. "Protective and Damaging Effects of Stress Mediators: Central Role of the Brain." *Dialogues in Clinical Neuroscience* 8 (4): 367–81.

———. 2013. "The Brain on Stress: Toward an Integrative Approach to Brain, Body and Behavior." *Perspectives on Psychological Science* 8 (6): 673–75.

———. 2016. "Epigenetic Interactions and the Brain-Body Communication." *Psychotherapy and Psychosomatics* 86 (1): 1–4.

Murray, Desiree, Katie Rosanbalm, Christina Christopoulos, and Amar Hamoudi. 2015. "Self-Regulation and Toxic Stress Report 1: Foundations for Understanding Self-Regulation from an Applied Perspective. OPRE Report #2015-21." Washington DC: Office of Planning, Research and Evaluation, Administration for Children and Families, U.S. Department of Health and Human Services.

National Education Alliance for Borderline Personality Disorder. 2024. "Overview of BPD." June 4, 2024. Accessed 27 November 2024. borderlinepersonalitydisorder.org.

National Health Service. 2021. "Complex PTSD -Post-Traumatic Stress Disorder." February 17, 2021. Accessed 11 Apr 2022. nhs.uk/mental-health/conditions.

National Institute on Alcohol Abuse and Alcoholism. 2007. "Alcohol Survey Reveals 'Lost Decade' between Ages of Disorder Onset and Treatment." 2 Jul 2007.

———. 2021. "Understanding Alcohol Use Disorder." April 2021.

National Scientific Council on the Developing Child. 2008. "The Timing and Quality of Early Experiences Combine to Shape Brain Architecture: Working Paper No. 5."

———. 2020. "Connecting the Brain to the Rest of the Body: Early Childhood Development and Lifelong Health Are Deeply Intertwined: Working Paper No. 15."

Neuroscience News. 2024. "How Childhood Trauma Alters Brain Pathways." February 5, 2024. Accessed 22 Jul 2024. neurosciencenews.com.

Nolan, Mark, Elena Roman, Anurag Nasa, Kirk J. Levins, Erik O'Hanlon, Veronica O'Keane, and Darren Willian Roddy. 2020. "Hippocampal and Amygdalar Volume Changes in Major Depressive Disorder: A Targeted Review and Focus on Stress." *Chronic Stress* 4 (January): 247054702094455.

O'Brien, Kathleen. 2015. "The First Adult Child of Alcoholics, She Was There from the Beginning." *NJ.com - The Star-Ledger*, June 3, 2015.

Palo Alto Weekly Staff. 2018. "Sheriff: Grisly 1974 Stanford Murder Solved." June 29, 2018.

Perry, Bruce, and Oprah Winfrey. 2021. *What Happened to You?: Conversations on Trauma, Resilience, and Healing*. New York: Flatiron Books.

Perry, Bruce. 2001. "The Neurodevelopmental Impact of Violence in Childhood." In *Textbook of Child and Adolescent Forensic Psychiatry*, edited by D. Schetky and E. P. Benedek. Washington DC: American Psychiatric Press.

———. 2017. "Trauma- and Stressor- Related Disorders in Infants, Children, and Adolescents." In *Textbook of Child and Adolescent Psychopathology, 3rd Ed.*, edited by T. P. Beauchaine and S. P. Hinshaw. New York: Wiley.

———. n.d. (in Press) "The Neurosequential Model." In *The Handbook of Therapeutic Child Care*, edited by J. Mitchell, J. Tucci, and E. Tronick. London: Jessica Kingsley.

Perry, Bruce, and Christine Dobson. 2013. "The Neurosequential Model of Therapeutics." In *Treating Complex Stress Disorders in Children and Adolescents*, edited by Julian Ford. New York: Guilford.

Perry, Bruce, and Maia Szalavitz. 2017. *The Boy Who Was Raised as a Dog*. New York: Basic Books.

Peterson, Carole. 2021. "What Is Your Earliest Memory? It Depends." *Memory* 29 (6): 1–12.

Polcari, Ann, Keren Rabi, Elizabeth Bolger, and Martin H. Teicher. 2014. "Parental Verbal Affection and Verbal Aggression in Childhood Differentially Influence Psychiatric Symptoms and Wellbeing in Young Adulthood." *Child Abuse & Neglect* 38 (1): 91–102.

Porges, Stephen W. 2017. *The Pocket Guide to Polyvagal Theory: The Transformative Power of Feeling Safe.* New York: W.W Norton.

———. 2021. "Polyvagal Theory: A Biobehavioral Journey to Sociality." *Comprehensive Psychoneuroendocrinology* 7 (June): 100069.

———. 1995. "Orienting in a Defensive World: Mammalian Modifications of Our Evolutionary Heritage." *Psychophysiology* 1995 Jul 32 (4):301-18.

Porter, Carly, Jasper Palmier-Claus, Alison Branitsky, Warren Mansell, Helen Warwick, and Filippo Varese. 2019. "Childhood Adversity and Borderline Personality Disorder: A Meta-Analysis." *Acta Psychiatrica Scandinavica* 141 (1): 6–20.

Pressfield, Steven, and Shawn Coyne. 2012. *Turning Pro.* New York: Black Irish Entertainment.

Putnam, Frank. 2006. "The Impact of Trauma on Child Development." *Juvenile and Family Court Journal* 57 (1): 1–11.

Raising Children Network. 2024. "Self-Regulation in Children and Teenagers." June 4, 2024. Accessed 24 Nov 2024. raisingchildren.net.au.

Reisz, Samantha, Robbie Duschinsky, and Daniel J. Siegel. 2017. "Disorganized Attachment and Defense: Exploring John Bowlby's Unpublished Reflections." *Attachment & Human Development* 20 (2): 107–34.

Repetti, Rena L., Shelley E. Taylor, and Teresa E. Seeman. 2002. "Risky Families: Family Social Environments and the Mental and Physical Health of Offspring." *Psychological Bulletin* 128 (2): 330–66.

Riesman, David, Nathan Glazer, Reuel Denney, Todd Gitlin, and Inc Ebrary. 2001. *The Lonely Crowd: A Study of the Changing American Character.* New Haven, CT: Yale University Press.

Robins, Lee. 1993. "Vietnam Veterans' Rapid Recovery from Heroin Addiction: A Fluke or Normal Expectation?" *Addiction* 88 (8):1041–54.

Robins, Lee N., Darlene H. Davis, and David N. Nurco. 1974. "How Permanent Was Vietnam Drug Addiction?" *American Journal of Public Health* 64 (12_Suppl): 38–43.

Rosanbalm, Katie, and Desiree Murray. 2017. "Co-Regulation from Birth through Young Adulthood: A Practice Brief, OPRE Brief #2017-80."

Washington DC: Office of Planning, Research, and Evaluation, Administration for Children and Families, US Department of Health and Human Services.

Sachs-Ericsson, Natalie, Edelyn Verona, Thomas Joiner, and Kristopher J. Preacher. 2006. "Parental Verbal Abuse and the Mediating Role of Self-Criticism in Adult Internalizing Disorders." *Journal of Affective Disorders* 93 (1-3): 71–78.

Salmon, Catherine, and Todd Shackelford. 2007. "Toward an Evolutionary Psychology of the Family." In *Family Relationships: An Evolutionary Perspective*, edited by Catherine Salmon and Todd Shackelford, pp 3-15. New York: Oxford University Press.

Satel, Sally, and Scott O. Lilienfeld. 2014. "Addiction and the Brain-Disease Fallacy." *Frontiers in Psychiatry* 4.

Schwartz, Arielle. 2020. *COMPLEX PTSD WORKBOOK: A Mind-Body Approach to Regaining Emotional Control and Becoming Whole*. Berkeley, CA: Althea Press.

———. 2021. "The Fawn Response in Complex PTSD." March 9, 2021. Accessed 12 Mar 2024. drarielleschwartz.com.

Seefeldt, Richard, and Mark Lyon. 1992. "Personality Characteristics of Adult Children of Alcoholics." *Journal of Counseling & Development* 70 (5): 588–93.

Sheline, Yvette I., Conor Liston, and Bruce S. McEwen. 2019. "Parsing the Hippocampus in Depression: Chronic Stress, Hippocampal Volume, and Major Depressive Disorder." *Biological Psychiatry* 85 (6): 436–38.

Shengold, Leonard. 1991. *Soul Murder: The Effects of Childhood Abuse and Deprivation*. New York: Ballantine Books.

Shonkoff, Jack, Andrew Garner, B. S. Siegel, M. I. Dobbins, M. F. Earls, A. S. Garner, L. McGuinn, J. Pascoe, and D. L. Wood. 2011. "The Lifelong Effects of Early Childhood Adversity and Toxic Stress." *Pediatrics* 129 (1): e232–46.

Sinclair, David. 2019. *Lifespan: Why We Age--and Why We Don't Have To*. New York: Atria Books.

Smith, Caleb. 2014. "Murder at Memorial Church Remains Unsolved 40 Years Later." *The Stanford Daily*, October 10, 2014.

Smith, Kyle. 2015. "Addiction Is Not a Disease — and We're Treating Addicts Incorrectly." *New York Post*, July 12, 2015.

Solis, Michael. 2020. "We Learn Faster When We Aren't Told What Choices to Make." *Scientific American*, October 1, 2020.

Spence, Joanne. 2021. *Trauma-Informed Yoga: A Toolbox for Therapists: 47 Simple Practices to Calm, Balance, and Restore the Nervous System*. Eau Claire, Wisconsin: Pesi Publishing.

Spitz, Rene A. 1945. "Hospitalism." *The Psychoanalytic Study of the Child* 1 (1): 53–74.

Straussner, Shulamith Lala Ashenberg. 2011. "Children of Substance-Abusing Parents: An Overview." In *Children of Substance-Abusing Parents*, edited by Christine Huff Fewell. New York: Springer.

Sullivan, Dan. 2024. "Unsatisfied with Your Progress? This Could Be Why." Strategic Coach. Accessed 26 Nov 2024. resources.strategiccoach.com.

Summit, Roland. 1983. "The Child Sexual Abuse Accommodation Syndrome." Child Abuse & Neglect. 7: 177–93.

Szalavitz, Maia. 2016. *Unbroken Brain*. New York: St. Martin's Press.

Tawwab, Nedra Glover. 2021. *Set Boundaries, Find Peace: A Guide to Reclaiming Yourself*. New York: Penguin.

Teicher, Martin H., Jeoffry B. Gordon, and Charles B. Nemeroff. 2021. "Recognizing the Importance of Childhood Maltreatment as a Critical Factor in Psychiatric Diagnoses, Treatment, Research, Prevention, and Education." *Molecular Psychiatry*, November.

Teicher, Martin H., Jacqueline A. Samson, Carl M. Anderson, and Kyoko Ohashi. 2016. "The Effects of Childhood Maltreatment on Brain Structure, Function and Connectivity." *Nature Reviews Neuroscience* 17 (10): 652–66.

Thayer, Zaneta, Celestina Barbosa-Leiker, Michael McDonell, Lonnie Nelson, Debra Buchwald, and Spero Manson. 2016. "Early Life Trauma, Post-Traumatic Stress Disorder, and Allostatic Load in a Sample of American Indian Adults." *American Journal of Human Biology* 29 (3).

The Decision Lab. 2022. "Why Do We Believe Misinformation More Easily When It's Repeated Many Times?" Accessed 11 Oct 2024. thedecisionlab.com.

Tolley, Rebecca. 2020. *A Trauma-Informed Approach to Library Services*. Chicago: ALA Editions.

Tomoda, Akemi, Yi-Shin Sheu, Keren Rabi, Hanako Suzuki, Carryl P. Navalta, Ann Polcari, and Martin H Teicher. 2011. "Exposure to Parental Verbal Abuse Is Associated with Increased Gray Matter Volume in Superior Temporal Gyrus." *NeuroImage* 54 Suppl 1: S280-6.

Tronick, Edward, and Bruce Perry. 2015. "Multiple Levels of Meaning-Making." In *Handbook of Body Therapy and Somatic Therapy*, edited by G. Marlock and H. Weiss. Berkeley, CA: North Atlantic Books.

U.S. Department of Health & Human Services, Administration for Children and Families, Administration on Children, Youth and Families, Children's Bureau. 2024. "Child Maltreatment 2022." Washington DC.

———. 2021. "Child Maltreatment 2019." Washington DC.

van der Kolk, Bessel van, Julian D. Ford, and Joseph Spinazzola. 2019. "Comorbidity of Developmental Trauma Disorder (DTD) and Post-Traumatic Stress Disorder: Findings from the DTD Field Trial." *European Journal of Psychotraumatology* 10 (1): 1562841.

Venegas, Alexandra, Suzanna Donato, Lindsay R. Meredith, and Lara A. Ray. 2021. "Understanding Low Treatment Seeking Rates for Alcohol Use Disorder: A Narrative Review of the Literature and Opportunities for Improvement." *The American Journal of Drug and Alcohol Abuse* 47 (6): 1-16.

Vicedo, M. 2010. "The Evolution of Harry Harlow: From the Nature to the Nurture of Love." *History of Psychiatry* 21 (2): 190-205.

Vicedo, M. 2009. "Mothers, Machines, and Morals: Harry Harlow's Work on Primate Love from Lab to Legend." *Journal of the History of the Behavioral Sciences* 45 (3): 193-218.

Walker, Pete. 2013. *Complex PTSD: From Surviving to Thriving: A Guide and Map for Recovering from Childhood Trauma*. Lafayette, CA: Azure Coyote.

———. 2017. HOMESTEADING in the CALM EYE of the STORM. Lafayette, CA: Azure Coyote.

Werner, Emmy E. 1993. "Risk, Resilience, and Recovery: Perspectives from the Kauai Longitudinal Study." *Development and Psychopathology* 5 (4): 503-15.

William Ian Miller. 1998. *The Anatomy of Disgust*. Cambridge, MA: Harvard University Press.

Winfrey, Oprah. 1993. "Conversations with Oprah: Andrew Vachss." July 16, 1993. Accessed 20 Nov 2024. oprah.com.

Wing, Nell. 1981. "Origin of the Serenity Prayer: A Historical Paper." Service Material from the General Service Office, Alcoholics Anonymous.

Winograd, Rachel Pearl, Douglas Steinley, and Kenneth Sher. 2015. "Searching for Mr. Hyde: A Five-Factor Approach to Characterizing 'Types of Drunks.'" *Addiction Research & Theory* 24 (1): 1–8.

Woititz, Janet. 1983. *Adult Children of Alcoholics*. Pompano Beach, FL: Health Communications.

———. 1990. *Adult Children of Alcoholics (Expanded Edition)*. Deerfield Beach, FL.: Health Communications.

Woititz, Lisa S. 2015. *Unwelcome Inheritance: Break Your Family's Cycle of Addictive Behaviors*. Minneapolis: Hazelden Information & Educational Services.

World Health Organization. 2019. "WHO Guidelines for the Health Sector Response to Child Maltreatment." Geneva: WHO.

www.ingramcontent.com/pod-product-compliance
Lightning Source LLC
Chambersburg PA
CBHW070723240426
43673CB00003B/120